Writing Your
Way Through
Cancer

Writing Your Way Through Cancer

CHIA MARTIN

HOHM PRESS
2000

Cover design: Kim Johansen
Layout and design: Visual Perspectives, Phoenix, Arizona

  Library of Congress Cataloging in Publication Data:
Martin, Chia.
     Writing your way through cancer / Chia Martin.
        p. cm.
     ISBN 1-890772-00-3 (alk. paper)
     1. Cancer—Patients—Diaries. 2. Creative writing—
        Therapeutic use. I. Title.

  RC262.M328 2000
  616.99'406515--dc21

                                                    00-025175

Poem on p. xi from *Cold Mountain: 100 Poems by the T'ang Poet Han-shan*, trans. Burton Watson. ©1970 Columbia University Press. Reprinted by permission of the publisher.

HOHM PRESS
P.O. Box 2501
Prescott, AZ 86302
800-381-2700
http://www.hohmpress.com

Printed in the U.S.A. on recycled paper using soy ink.

For Father and Son

Acknowledgments

My deepest gratitude to: my healing team who have gone beyond the confines of limited thinking to support me on my healing journey: Frank Iorio, M.D., Deborah Lindquist, M.D., Robert Myers, N.D., Mary Shackelton, N.D., Paula Zuccarello, Nachama Greenwald, Starr Fuentes and Deborah Auletta—the Diva—for her tireless service, and the late Dr. Hans Nieper, a true healer.

My editor, Regina Sara Ryan, for encouraging me to write my own truth.

Becky Fulker for decoding my handwritten manuscript without complaint.

My brother Tom for his unconditional love.

Debbie Hogeland, the living expression of generosity and selfless service.

My beautiful family, whose sweet smiles of compassion shower me every day.

My teacher, Lee Lozowick, who continues to bless and guide each and every step on this sacred path.

Author's Note

This book contains many samples of my own writing. Their purpose is to serve as examples of and testimonies to the possibility of *Writing Your Way Through Cancer*. The choices revealed in my writing are *my choices*. Your choices are yours. No choices or opinions reflected here are meant to be used in a medically diagnostic or prescriptive fashion. This book is not another offbeat "cure" for cancer. It is a manual for writing as a tool for living with cancer.

Contents

Introduction   xiii

Part I: Some Ideas for Recording Your Journey   xvii
     Creative Expression as a Legitimate Healer   1
     Why Write   3
     The "How" of Writing   7
     A Few Words on Poetry   17
     Dialogues   24
     Letter Writing   26
     The Importance of Dreams   29
     Dumping   33
     Follow Your Heart   35
     Let It Write You   39

Part II: Writing Through the Stages   43
  1. Coping With Cancer   43
     Shock   46
     Treatment   53
     Pain   59
     Denial   64
     Anger   69
     Fear   73

  2. Living With Cancer   79
     Resilience   83
     Affirmations   88
     Visualizations   95

Contents

Telling the Story   101
Language   106
Cultivating Silence   111
The Space Between   113
Celebration   116
Humor   120

3. **Transforming Through Cancer**   123
    Dignity   126
    Waiting   131
    Loneliness, Aloneness, Solitude   134
    Prayer   138
    Service   142
    Rebirth   145
    Forgiveness   150
    Death is Not a Failure   153

4. **The Unknown**   157
    The Mystery   160
    Ravishment   165

Would you know a simile for life and death?
Compare them then to water and ice.
Water binds together to become ice;
Ice melts and turns back to water.
What has died must live again,
What has been born shall return to death.
Water and ice do no harm to each other;
Life and death are both of them good.

—Han-shan, from *Cold Mountain Poems*

Introduction

In April of 1998 I had a colonoscopy to determine what might be causing the chronic diarrhea I had experienced for years. I went home in a state of shock—a large tumor was discovered in the colon. My doctor was ninety-nine percent sure it was cancer. There was no question that surgery was necessary. The post-surgery pathology report confirmed adenocarcinoma with positive lymph involvement. The following December a chest x-ray revealed metastatic bilateral lung lesions.

As I have sometimes struggled, sometimes soared, through the ups and downs of living with cancer, I have found that writing can caress my wounds, encourage my tears, shout my anger, uncover my fears and invoke my prayers. It has been my most trusted confidante and guide through both the darkest corners of hell and the highest peaks of heaven.

Writing my way through cancer has given me something much more reliable than hope. It has been the primary vehicle through which I have begun to learn that life is quite simply just what it is. Through my writing I am gradually learning to cease asking why, for the "whys" are unimportant, as are the "whens" and "how longs." I have begun to grasp the truth that I am not in charge and that death is not a failure. This last year I have never been more aware of the fact that every life on earth is here both to *be* a lesson as well as *learn* a lesson. It is through listening with attention that we are able to hear the lessons of our own hearts and the hearts of others. Writing is about listening. Listening is about healing. Healing is about an embracing of what is that far surpasses cure.

This book is an expression of my gratitude for the gift of cancer—the gift of writing. I hope it can offer you an avenue into your own healing journey.

Writing Your Way Through Cancer is a process of self-discovery, an invitation into your unique healing journey. You needn't be an experienced writer to find help here. In Part I, Some Ideas for Recording Your Journey, you will find simple tips, springboard ideas and helpful reminders to assist in beginning a writing practice. Start small; even ten minutes a day will produce sizable benefits. If the thought of finding the time to write is overwhelming in addition to what may already be a staggering regime, try writing instead of watching TV, reading the newspaper, engaging in energy-draining phone conversations, surfing the Internet, snacking or merely *thinking* about writing. A helpful guideline for all healing activity, including writing, is that when facing choices opt for the life supportive, health supportive alternatives.

If you already have an established writing practice, hopefully *Writing Your Way Through Cancer* will be a catalyst for sharper self-observation and reflection, friendly encouragement for experimentation, and welcome permission to explore the ocean of mystery that cancer presents.

Writing can be done just about anywhere. I suggest choosing a space that lends itself to supporting your healing. Honor your writing practice by bringing a sacred mood to it. You might wish to purchase a blank book and new pen or you might find a legal pad best suits your needs. My personal credos are: *Simple is best* and *Follow your intuition.*

Regardless of the stage of your cancer, writing is a unique tool for assisting in your healing. I think of healing as a vital process which considers the whole being: physical, emotional and spiritual. Healing is about growth and change. It is fluid and, most importantly, cannot be qualified or stifled by judgments such as right or wrong, good or bad. Healing includes the full spectrum of life and its prism of challenge: joy and sorrow, anger and gratitude, pain and acceptance. Healing does not have cure as its goal. In fact, healing continues beyond remission, survival, cure, and even death.

Part II, Writing Your Way Through the Stages, is divided into four sections: Coping with Cancer, Living with Cancer, Transforming Through Cancer and The Unknown. It is a compilation of essays, journal entries and poems written as part of my own cancer healing. Hopefully they will inspire you to record similar experiences and encourage you to venture into areas that are very different from mine.

Writing Your Way Through Cancer lends itself to myriad uses. You may wish to read it straight through, reflecting on the common threads in cancer healing, then return to it as a reference source for your own writing practice. You may prefer to read Part I to establish a matrix for *Writing Your Way Through Cancer,* then skip about in Part II as you encounter the particular issues it covers. Keep the book nearby for easy reference, especially when you are faced with a tough treatment choice or disappointing lab report, when you have an insight into an unresolved conflict or an encounter with fear. I hope you will discover, as I have, that writing about these and other issues of your healing can lead you into the domain of wisdom and acceptance.

Part I

Some Ideas For
Recording Your Journey

Creative Expression as a Legitimate Healer

Before I gave birth to my daughter I was an avid journal writer. I was rarely without my journal. It was not uncommon to find me writing just about anywhere. I've pulled out my journal in a Memphis blues club, a café in Berlin, the powder room of the Taj Mahal Hotel in Bombay, in airports, airplanes, buses, taxis, on street corners, in cathedrals, cemeteries and surgical recovery rooms.

After my daughter was born my journaling virtually ceased. It seemed that the time I had spent writing was now consumed with all the joyous and challenging tasks of a new mother. I wanted desperately to write about all the wonder and mystery of that time, but every time I picked up my pen I nodded out instead.

One night, during a nursing marathon, it dawned on me that the internal substance I had previously defined as my "creative juice" was literally pouring out of my breasts, straight into my daughter's mouth. An almost identical mood was present during breast-feeding that had been present while writing.

That realization has remained with me for many years. Of course I am no longer breast-feeding a child, however I am as deeply engaged in sustaining the life of my healing process. In my experience, real creative expression is innately healing. I have read numerous accounts of people plagued with chronic pain of one kind or another, cata-strophic illness, paralyzation or other forms of impairment who have literally found that their pain was managed, their suffering lightened, their disease spontaneously healed by diving headlong into one form of creative expression or another.

And so, I write, and encourage you to write too.

Why Write?

- Writing strengthens the immune system. According to research conducted by James W. Pennebaker, Ph.D., people who wrote about upsetting experiences showed improvement in immune system function. (James W. Pennebaker, Ph.D., *Opening Up*, New York, 1990, William Morrow and Co.)

- Writing encourages uninhibited expression. There's no censor. Anything goes from cursing and yelling to bargaining and praying.

- Writing objectifies our experience. It's so tempting to keep cancer as a personal nightmare, full of horrific creatures who are out to get us. Writing our experiences coaxes these dark-dwelling monsters of our mind out into the light of reality allowing us to see their true nature.

- Writing is a medicine that delivers a very powerful message to the cells. Whenever we speak our own *truth*—either verbally or through our writing—we are literally infusing our body with the medicine of this truth. What could be more healing?

- Writing generates personal power. Writing about my cancer journey has strengthened my trust in my own sense of what is best for my healing more than any other treatment I have engaged. It has been a relentless coach sometimes, but I am no longer afraid to question authority and to say no if I need to.

- Writing stimulates a mood of healing, and the written piece itself is the proof this mood has taken place.

- Writing enables us to de-stress in a typically stressful situation.

- Writing is a tool for integrating physical, emotional and spiritual-healing.

- Writing is a doorway into insight and personal introspection.

- Writing clears the mind. Time has become very precious since my diagnosis. Priorities have shifted, encouraging me to set boundaries that support managing my time wisely. This process includes managing my mental activity. I am virtually unwilling to engage in "mental masturbation"—playing and replaying an uncomfortable conversation, misunderstanding or apology in my mind. I write my experience, clear the mind and move on.

- Writing is free and can be done almost anywhere by anyone.

- Writing teaches us discrimination. I have frequently driven home from a doctor's appointment, treatment session, or visit for tea with a friend with a funny feeling about a treatment recommendation, diagnostic opinion, or well-intended but patronizing speech. Writing quickly brings me back to my center and allows me to retain what was/is of value in my healing, and what is not.

From My Journal

October 1998

I am aware of how important it is to keep writing now and to not be afraid of fear. To explain a little: I have recently observed that I have been cultivating (to a small degree but I don't want it to grow!) a fear that if I encounter fear of recurrence, weakness, tiredness, weight loss, etc., the fear will feed negative view and then give permission or encouragement for those things to happen. Consequently, it became rather obvious that I was systematically avoiding fear rather than observing or feeling it, accepting it and finally surrendering it.

The avoidance is all part of the perfectionist disposition. The pure willingness to practice, not give "it" any energy, stay positive and so forth is all wonderful and even admirable. However, avoiding or stuffing or even ignoring the fear can be dangerous and eventually lead to creating (perhaps) the opposite effect than I had planned.

This dawned on me last week in relationship to an increasing pain I have had in my left hip. The pain was there prior to my surgery, and it was apparent that it was a muscle-skeletal type thing. Quite frankly, awareness of this pain was subsumed by the discovery of the tumor and all the health care surrounding that. The pain did not go away, but simply dimmed in the light of much deeper pain.

However, over the last month as my body has gotten stronger, I have been aware of how much my hip is hurting and how badly it hurt all summer. I was hoping the pain would simply resolve itself. During an exam, the doctor noticed me favoring the hip and asked, rather intuitively and pointedly, what the problem was. Boom! The minute he asked I saw my fear flash before my face. I asked with the voice of a child: "Are there lymph glands in there?" "Yes there are," he answered patiently. "However, they are very deep. It's unlikely you would feel them." After examining it he concluded that the muscle had taken on stress in relationship to the tumor growth, surgery and trauma.

"Fear of recurrence," he reminded me, "is a natural thing. I've never known a cancer patient not experience it. And it may go on for a long time. You can't let it be a motivating factor to hide." After speaking it, the pain subsided, the fear diminished. One of the biggest tasks I have at present is to let the fear of recurrence arise and simply pass by like a movie playing itself out in my mind.

The "How" of Writing

As I noted in the Introduction, some of you will be experienced writers, some will be approaching for the first time. The following suggestions are intended to provide a supportive framework in which to integrate *Writing Your Way Through Cancer* into your daily rhythm. There was a time when the mere thought of writing catapulted me into such insecurity and self-doubt that I was paralyzed. These tips are both tricks and friendly companions I have used to get me going and keep me steady in my writing practice.

- You have something to say. It is unique, authentic, solely yours. There is no right or wrong. Even two people with an identical diagnosis will obviously have different life experiences. When you read my story its uniqueness is the blend of my feelings, insights and challenges. Allow your story to reveal you.

- As mentioned earlier, honor your writing practice by bringing a sacred mood to it. Select your writing implements, journaling books and other invocational tools such as candles and incense with care. I use a Dr. Grip™ pen and spiral bound lined notebooks or journals. They tend to be easier to lay flat. However, in my own healing, softening my rigid "have-to" edges has been important, so I make a point of using any and every decorative journal I am gifted with, no matter how awkward. I also use yellow legal pads for the first drafts of poems, and elementary school copy books to record second copies of certain pieces. Remember, simple and cheap is fine!

- The benefits reaped from most things are a direct result of the amount of time and attention we give to them. In order to truly experience the inestimable value of writing as a tool for healing with cancer we must put in the time. The amount of time is not really important. I've found it's the quality of attention and the consistency that matters most. Bringing consistency to any aspect of our healing will exponentially increase the possibility of the practice being a positive contributor to overall well-being.

- Unless you have already cultivated a writing practice you will need to build what I have come to term your writing muscle. As with any physical exercise, dietary regime or other self-care program, there is no substitute for consistency. If you can manage to write a paragraph or a poem each day—do it. As a result you may discover a writing habit/muscle developing very quickly. This habit can then be easily integrated into your daily rhythm. Sometimes the tone of the muscle is maintained by stretching a little beyond your limit. For instance, I have discovered a tendency in myself to jump up and straighten the rug just when I'm on the brink of vulnerability or intense confrontation in my writing practice. In this case, stretching urges me to resist avoiding these uncomfortable feelings. At other times the body needs the safety found in a reliable rhythm. Please remember that if you miss a day, or even a few days, simply pick up where you left off.

- Although writing may confront an array of deep and often intense emotions, it should not become a source of stress. Permission to write without censoring, with relaxation and inner listening are key to moving through creative blocks or times when writing is virtually impossible, for example, during chemotherapy intervals. If you find a longing to write during these periods, but are too weak or ill with side effects, try keeping a notepad close by. You may feel enlivened or comforted by being able to simply jot down a thought or word that you can come back to later when you feel stronger. If you are comfortable with your caregiver or friend supporting your writing practice, you might also try dictating your thoughts to him/her.

Writing cannot be healing if used to *guilt* yourself. In order for writing to be transformative, it must be treated with respect, not as yet another "medicine" we must take on in our battle against cancer.

• There are no mistakes in this writing process. Mistakes are the concern of a perfectionistic society. Certainly you want to put thought and elegance into your writing. However, *Writing Your Way Through Cancer* is primarily a vehicle for self-discovery and healing. Mistakes are the compost that nourishes a newly planted garden. Mistakes are a very important window into your healing process. Welcome the opportunity to learn from them.

• There are no lost thoughts. If you had the thought once, you can have it again. Too often we are seduced by the mind into believing that if we neglect to write something down soon after it happened we will never be able to enter into that possibility again. My own experience proves this theory to be false time and again. In fact, sometimes we aren't ready to write about an experience until it is fully integrated.

An easy way to trick the mind is to return to the experience in your imagination. Then as rapidly as you can, without any considering or editing, jot down every word that arises. Sooner or later the trigger word will present itself, and your pen will be off and running. I wrote the poem on page 108 about my scar a year and a half after my cancer surgery, two years after my hysterectomy, and nine years after my cesarean.

- As you write make notations of any *gems* you wish to return to and explore further. You may find, as I have, that you can strengthen your healing by expounding on the gem of a new feeling, a sweet memory, a powerful realization. In addition on days when you want to write but feel "stuck," pull out a gem and shine it up.

- I am going to be really old-fashioned here and proclaim that there is no substitute for the value of writing in longhand. Period. First of all, sitting in front of a computer screen is not the healthiest spot for someone working with cancer. It is my opinion that returning as much as possible to organic activity is crucial to our healing. Pen and paper is definitely more organic than a cathode-ray computer terminal. Secondly, longhand writing keeps you in touch with your body. (For the record, this book was written entirely in longhand!)

- Don't be afraid to tell it like it is. Take risks. Writing from the heart demands we take risks. Taking risks in our writing will help us take risks in other areas of our healing, thus confronting fear, crystallized attitudes, and other life negative habits we may have become comfortable with. *It's your experience.* You needn't take care of the doctor's feelings, your mother-in-law's reputation or your father's abuse. Of course, if you plan to publish then the game changes, but most of us will choose to write our way through cancer in the privacy of our own journals. A caution: taking risks is different from ranting, dumping and complaining. (See section on Dumping, page 33.)

- Often we have crystal clear realizations in times of shock, intense pain or loss. These realizations can be elusive in nature—so much so that when we try to resurrect them in times of fear, anger or need they are nowhere to be found, somehow concealed in the recesses of the subconscious. *Writing Your Way Through Cancer* can be a very effective technique for recording these realizations. Then you can return to them when the chips are down and you need self-encouragement.

- *Writing Your Way Through Cancer* cannot have "best seller" as its focus or goal. When we write with this mentality we tend to compromise the quality of our writing practice. *Writing Your Way Through Cancer* has the possibility of tapping into the source of our creativity so that everyday journaling becomes a journey into the sacred. In order for this to take place, we must let go of any overly dramatic tendencies to make our journal or our story into our swan song. This will actually dilute its authentic power. It is highly unlikely that some final, dramatic victory or success, like having a journal read and loved by millions, is going to bring the boost to our healing we may be seduced into hoping it will. In fact, these motivations are often cure-oriented, fueled with the inherent risk of breeding false hope.

- Do not limit your journaling or writing to the domain of cancer. Hopefully *Writing Your Way Through Cancer* will serve as a catalyst and inspiration for a variety of written expressions to blossom forth.

- Write for the sake of writing, and the writing will write you.

From My Journal

December 1998

I've been contemplating a significant and evolving change in relationship to food since my surgery. I've had time to reflect on the exquisite delight I have taken in cooking for loved ones. And oh the meals I have designed and either executed myself or assisted others in executing over the years! Goose with beets and roquefort; traditional Thanksgiving dinner replete with cornbread stuffing, candied yams and southern pecan pie; for our French guests, caviar and champagne; huevos rancheros for 100; seven course Chinese; an authentic Biblical feast; a Middle Eastern market under a tent.

I have insinuated myself into the kitchens of India, Germany, France and Los Angeles (including Wolfgang Puck's). I have taken cooking classes with Jacques Pepin, Deborah Madison and Barbara Fenzl. I've read Julia Child's biography, Laurie Colwin's letters and Gerald Asher's articles on every aspect of wine one can imagine. I've watched Paul Prudhomme, Julia, Pierre Franey, and Madhur Jaffrey cook on TV for twenty-five years. "Babette's Feast"—well, what can I say . . .

I've dreamed menus for kings, queens, presidents, screen stars, and gurus. While recovering from surgery my bored mind has spent hours planning the most amazing banquets, kaiseki dinners, southern Bar-B-Ques, church suppers, wine tastings, chocolate extravaganzas, tailgate picnics, Pooh tea parties, breakfasts-in-bed, candlelight dinners for two, high teas, pre-football cookouts for a gang of teenagers, and every kind of food gift.

I have romanced a relationship with food for thirty-five years. This romance has deepened, ripened and matured. It's gained dimension. I don't mean to imply here, in any way whatsoever, that I am knowledgeable or skilled. In fact, as I have written before—I am not a very good cook at all. I just have a passion for food as an invocational tool, and particularly the way flavors, colors, and textures all harmonize to create a gift to and expression of God's glory.

I love to read cookbooks and cooking magazines. I like to study recipes and other types of information on food and wine. I never tire of shopping for ingredients, especially in open-air markets, gourmet stores and restaurant supply houses. Ethnic markets are a thrill.

At this point I am wondering why I would be writing about all this in my "cancer" journal. Why? Because my diet now and most likely forever is limited, to say the least. The things I need to eat—as close to daily as possible—are: millet, seaweed, green leafy vegetables, fresh carrot juice, pumpkin, broccoli, sprouts, green tea, flax oil. The things I need to exclude are: meat, poultry, seafood, eggs, caffeine, sugar, honey, white flour, excess dairy, most dried fruit, apples and apple juice. (Two very different worlds, and yet two worlds that can intersect.)

This cancer diet has indeed turned my head back to the essence of my lover, the actual source of the passion for food. Once this summer in France, walking through the open market in LaRoche Posay, I rejoiced to see the vendors with their fresh goat cheeses, homemade sausage, racks of lovely brown hen's eggs, samples of local wine, jars of honey with the honeycomb glistening inside. Of course the most seductive stalls were the portable bakeries—baguettes of every size and shape, country loaves and confections to make the heart skip a beat. And last but never least, the delicious ice cream and the aisles of French chocolate.

I remember so clearly that day, looking at all these wonderful foods and feeling a void inside where the rush of excitement at seeing one's lover in the flesh used to be. I looked in this corner and that, imagining that my thrill was simply playing hide and seek. No luck. On the grossest psychological level I deduced it was simply an issue of sour grapes—I couldn't eat any of these delectable morsels anymore, so I wasn't interested. Although that seemed the most likely explanation, somehow there seemed to be more to it than that.

I stopped in front of the chevré stall replete with samples for the taking and reached inside to the place where romance used to be. It seemed empty. Right there, with an ash covered dome of pure white chevré begging me to taste her creamy insides, I realized I felt like a jilted lover. Of course, in reality, "food" as I had known it before my surgery had not abandoned me. It was I who had chosen to turn away, to refuse the generously offered taste. It was I who had to say no to recklessly slathering a hunk of baguette with fresh butter. It was I who must pass the platter stacked high with French pastry or say no to the hand offering a chunk of dark glistening chocolate. All of a sudden I had this feeling of being in an arranged marriage with a new husband: chard, millet and sprouts.

Of course it's not as though these healing foods were so different from the diet I normally eat, which is wholesome, organic, fresh and in season. The revelation was that I had been married to this everyday diet (which I love) all the while having a torrid affair with butter, cream, sugar. Plainly put, I wanted to continue my juicy game. And I knew and know that I cannot. Not in that way. It is imperative that I maintain the diet recommended for the prevention of colon cancer. It is imperative for many reasons, the possible cost to not maintaining it being immediate and obvious.

Through this process, as with everything else that has come my way the last year, I am grateful to say that the actual passion has grown and changed for the better. One of the reasons being that the passion is actually about context, not content. It's about hospitality and the laws that govern that hospitality. It's about a holy relationship to the essence of an almond, the shape of a pear, God's gift in a grain of rice. It's about simplicity and reverence, prayer and thanksgiving for the gift of our Daily Bread.

I feel that God is using this opportunity to refine something in me and to actually expand what was previously a limited perspective, even though it would seem the opposite because the diet has gone from expansion to limitation. Yet another illusion. My experience is that the limitation of actual food substances has created expansion in context, or perhaps more accurately, inner possibility.

I'm thrilled with the opportunity to fall in love again with the simplicity of a beet, the greenness of a piece of chard, the aroma of a pineapple, the texture of millet, the miracle of aramé. This call to refinement ostensibly for health reasons has gifted me with the opportunity to investigate sacred ritual in relationship to food on a much simpler scale.

When I prepare my green tea in the morning I attempt to bring as much gratitude and sacred prayer to this as possible. I honor the ginger. I try to remember, even if it's really only a fleeting thought, that green tea has a heritage. It's part of a sacred tradition that has been honored for centuries. I also acknowledge through both prayer and intention that this same tea is an antioxidant and enemy of cancer. There's ruthlessness in this tea. I care for my teapot and bowl with reverence. Through my practice of restrictive diet, God has placed me in a position of being able to receive these gifts of attention.

Invocational cooking has little to do with butter, cream, sugar and wine. Although invocational cooking might indeed include these fancy ingredients, it is not based on these or any other ingredients. Isn't it a fact that all the highest forms of spiritual practice are contained in something as simple as the way one cuts the melon; the way one slices a tomato; the way one washes a head of lettuce, minces parsley or peels garlic? I have floated into rapture while stirring a pot of the simplest tomato garlic soup. I have *remembered to allow my tears to transform into tears of longing when cutting red onions.*

And now I have so many glorious possibilities available that I can't keep up with them. From remembering that abstinence can be a welcomed choice (not just a function of deprivation) when passing on dessert, to truly stopping before eating a bite of millet to remember that all of God's universe is contained in even one grain. At times I may indeed still feel like a jilted lover and ache for a slice of the most decadent chocolate torte in all of France. But, I can also find that same mistress in the juice of an orange.

"The tendency of ordinary cooks is to handle plain food carelessly and rich food carefully. As one practicing the buddhadharma, you should prepare food with all the ardor of your life and with wholehearted sincerity."

From *Refining Your Life* by Dogen and Uchiyama (New York: Weatherhill, 1983, p. 49)

A Few Words on Poetry

Writing poetry is an integral element of *Writing Your Way Through Cancer*. It has immense healing power. Because it is the language of the heart, poetry invites spaciousness and vulnerability. Thoughts or feelings we may find awkward or intimidating to work with can be the basis of an entire poem. Poetry gives voice to our unconscious. It is often a song through which cancer, pain, grief and celebration can sing. If you encounter trepidation, fear, even prejudice about writing poetry, begin there. For example, your first lines could be:

I am not a poet
But I do have cancer
Perhaps I fear writing poetry
As much as I fear cancer

Many of us are afraid of poetry, finding ourselves bound by the definitions of poetry we encountered in school. But, as far as I'm concerned, you needn't know anything about poetry or the "great" poets in order to write your own poetry. In fact, the metaphor and symbolism in Blake and Shelley may stand as barriers to poetic expression rather than serve as examples of one form of poetry.

Poetry is very forgiving. It encourages risk-taking. Punctuation rules can be cast aside. Grammar is open ended, thus allowing the poet as well as the cancer patient to let go and express. I have been able to write about sorrow, grief, jealousy, determination, gratitude, rage, forgiveness, isolation and much more through my poetry—subjects I found more difficult to express in prose.

- With your poetry you may want to write a rough draft to work with before copying the final form.

- Remember, your poetry is your *gift* to yourself.

- Creating stress over your writing is not conducive to healing.

- Explore the realms of humor and pathos.

- If you want to take on a different challenge, try haiku.

- Experiment with rhyming and meter.

- Finally, real listening is the key. When the heart speaks, the soul can hear if we stop, take a break, and listen. You may be pleasantly surprised, comforted, confronted, and at times even shocked by what you hear.

CT Scan

Cold
Still
Quiet
So quiet
Like being in the wilderness
In snow

Almost imperceptible movement
Rocking
Prenatal
A cold womb
Icy cold

Shallow breath
Almost meditative
Except for
Robot voice
Interrupting the softness

The rocking
The smell of radiation
Reminder of tumors

Glaciers
That sink ships
Swallow lives
In their frozen waters
Without remorse

Shivering
Chanting
Rocking
Waiting
For the warmth of God's arms

From My Journal

April 1998
pre-surgery/pre-diagnosis

I went for a CT scan last week. The scan itself was not so awful. However, drinking the three full glasses of barium has to be one of the single most nauseating experiences yet. Oh my God . . . what yuck, yuck, yuck!

For this test I didn't have to fast all night or do enemas. I simply couldn't have anything to eat or drink (including water) from 10:00 A.M., until all was complete around 3:00 P.M. or so. It was a shaky night so I was fantastically thirsty—parched. I can't remember when I have appreciated nor wanted water more. When I arrived at the lab I was given two large glasses of barium to drink and told to return in one hour. Unfortunately you're not escorted to some quiet private place to consume this delicious elixir. No, you have to sit in a claustrophobic waiting area with everybody and their brother (or sister) watching you gag, hold your nose, shiver and try everything imaginable to keep from throwing up.

Rita, who was my escort and advocate, walked me to the lobby where we paged my dear friend and nurse, Carmen. She took us to a lovely sitting room which was normally reserved for family and friends of emergency room patients. It was empty so I was able to lie down on a comfy couch and rest, aware that actually it was not the night's sleeplessness that was exhausting but rather the immense effort required to keep down the barium.

There was a VCR and TV monitor in this room as well. After resting a bit I got up and looked in the video cabinet somehow hoping to find a Steve Martin comedy. How naive . . . The drawer was full of videos, oh yes it was. Catch these titles: "The Cancer Patient"; "Cancer in the Family";

"The Complete Breast Cancer Video"; "Cancer and You." I slammed the drawer shut and returned to the couch to wait.

Finally, the lab technician calls my name. She is young, attractive and all smiles, which is actually helpful. We chat a bit on the walk to the lab. She shows me into a dressing room, explains how to put on the gown and so forth. Then the clincher! While she's doing her schtick I notice an identical glass full of barium sitting on the bench next to the complicated gown that awaits. I try to ignore it, averting my eyes to her big bright smile. I'm thinking, "This cannot be for real, nor for me. They didn't say anything about another glass of this poison." Up to this point she hasn't said a word about it. Then there's a pregnant pause, after which she says, "And when you're all dressed . . . "

I interrupt pointing to the devil drink, "That is a joke, isn't it?"

"No," she candidly answers. "It's all for you."

"Maybe the guy before me left it behind . . . " I plead chuckling a bit. I'm secretly hoping a sense of humor is going to somehow make this bad dream go away.

"No," she says again. "It's all yours. Hold your nose, close your eyes and drink it down. All of it."

"They don't tell you out there you're gonna have to do another one while you're trying to keep from throwing up the first two!" I quip.

"Yes," she says, "I know. I think we do that on purpose or people might not ever go through with it," she laughs.

I drink it down and move into a room in which the temperature has to be kept at 65° or so. The CT machine is definitely imposing. Huge, white, spic-n-span—a very sterile atmosphere. The technician explains how it works—there will be a computer voice telling me what to do. She will do a few rounds of x-rays, then put in an IV of dye which will make a contrast. "It will make you feel warm and flushed in the chest. That's normal. You may also feel as if you're going to pee all over but you won't. That's normal, too." I think to myself, is any of this normal?

The young woman explains that she'll be giving me a small enema at the end of the whole procedure to dye the lower part of the colon. But when she immediately comes over to insert the enema tip I realize that I have this stuck up my rectum for the next forty-five minutes. Oh joy! Poked, pulled, messed with . . .

So the scan begins. I almost fall asleep. Something about this machine is actually very relaxing. I think about Tibetan bardos *(transitional stages in the soul's journey between life and death), and the doctrine which suggests that some* bardos *are pleasant, others not so. This could be training for traveling in the "not so" I surmise.*

The technician does a few trial x-rays. The whole thing is a rather interesting, curious experience. I could do with a real voice instead of the robot, however. Another blanket would be nice too. Maybe a little Bach piped in...a few human touches. Oh well.

Next comes the IV. My best vein, which is in my right arm, was still sore from the IV inserted for the colonoscopy. The doctor attributed the extreme pain to a valium burn in the vein. She would need to find another vein.

Poke. "Sorry." Poke. "Ooh, sorry." She pulls out the needle explaining that she'll have to call in an IV expert. Enema tip still in place. No she can't take it out.

Shortly, two nurses appear. We joke a little while they discuss their strategy. "Could I have another blanket please?" The new nurse feels this vein and that. Here we go.

Poke. So far so good, I'm thinking. Poke. Uh oh, poke deeper. Ouch! This is starting to really hurt. I'm so thirsty. All the while this is going on I am using visualization. I imagine my veins as lovely streams, crystalline waters gently flowing freely through open channels. I stroke them tenderly with my thoughts. I apologize for the intrusion, the assault. I thank them for giving so freely time and again to what seems an endless brigade of needles.

"I'm so sorry," the nurse grimaces. "The vein just collapsed. Bring me some hot compresses from ER," she says to her partner. She wraps my arm in about eight hot towels. I lay there praying softly, silently, while they gossip and carry on about their work. Another try.

"Are you ready?" she asks.

"Sure," I answer. "Go ahead."

"Bingo," she says. "It's in."

Out they march. I feel the dye warming me. It's a distinct feeling but not unpleasant. I feel strangely altered. Almost in bliss. I think God is blessing me with this openness in the face of it all. There are no thoughts, no fear, no pressure.

"Boy you sure are a good sport," she says as she releases the fluid in the enema bag. Back under the scan I go on this automated table. "Breathe . . . hold it . . . now breathe" drones the robot's voice over and over again. "Okay," the nurse grants. "You're done. You can go to the toilet now." I look up out of this inward turning. All I can think of is a drink of water.

Dialogues

Written dialogues can be an effective tool for *Writing Your Way Through Cancer*. Dialogues afford the possibility of having a conversation with *yourself* that you might be either too inhibited or distracted to have otherwise. Dialogues can be held between different parts of your psyche. They can be between you and others—the difference being, of course, *you* get to speak all the parts. You can have a running conversation with God, with your cancer or with death.

Dialogues are a clever means of stimulating insight. For example, through a dialogue with your father about your choice to quit your job as a senior partner in a law firm following a diagnosis of prostate cancer, you may discover a previously unexamined fear of failure, misguided ambition, or other wounds that can begin to heal, thus influencing your overall well being. In this case a written dialogue might help strengthen your intention to live your life differently, as well as aid in reclaiming your personal power in relation to your father.

Before choosing treatment you might write out the dialogue you anticipate between yourself and your doctor. Perhaps after years of engaging holistic medicine you are considering chemotherapy. Try writing an anticipated dialogue between yourself and your healthcare practitioner. Such an exercise will encourage you to examine your choices, as well as strengthen your intuitive sense of your own healing process *before* feeling "put on the spot," which can lead to defensiveness and confusion. After you actually have that meeting, refer back to the written dialogue. It will give you objective feedback around your projections, fears, denial and false expectations. Conversely, it may confirm your sense that prejudices sometimes inform recommendations from even the most trusted family doctor.

Dialoguing can be a shortcut out of the cul-de-sac of victimization and self-pity. In line with this, another extremely effective dialogue is to ask your cancer what lesson it has come to teach you. Writing such a conversation can be quite revealing. You not only write it, you have to read it. More than once I have re-read a piece of writing to hear myself inquire, "Gee, is that really how I feel?" Another dialoguing technique is to write the way you *usually* respond followed by the way you *intend* to respond.

Try writing a dialogue in which you tell your children, parents, ex-husband or new friend (male or female) about your diagnosis. Observe any tendency to apologize, dramatize or retreat into denial. Blame, justification and resentment also become visible in written dialogues. Keep in mind that in written dialogues you can write the responses you hope for, which can also be quite revealing. Although I felt clarity in my desire not to be pitied around my diagnosis, through a written dialogue I was forced to see that I definitely desired sympathy (and plenty of it) from my mother. As a result, I was able to confront this unhealthy pattern which still had life, write my way through it, and manifest something different when I did eventually tell my mother about my cancer.

Letter Writing

Unfortunately the Art of Letters seems to be a dinosaur that's slowly being buried under the mounting sands of e-mail. I love the Art of Letters. I adore fine stationery and handmade papers. I derive great aesthetic pleasure in selecting the perfect paper to function as a canvas for my correspondence. Being one of those people who has never cultivated a taste for talking on the phone, and shudders at the thought of Internet intimacy, I have acquired a rich and fulfilling body of correspondence. There is simply no exchange for the organic joy inherent in pulling an engraved envelope out of the mailbox, checking the return address with anticipation, waiting for just the right moment, carefully slicing open the envelope, slipping out a crisp piece of linen paper that conceals a few dried rose petals, and venturing into the world that my loved ones and I share.

In *Writing Your Way Through Cancer* there are two basic forms your letters can take—sent and unsent. Each has tremendous and distinct value. One of the greatest advantages of letter writing is that you can speak without interruption. Sharing our cancer experience with loved ones can be intense and frightening as well as gratifying and freeing. Corresponding through letters may allow for a vulnerability that is stressful in person. Many of us don't have the luxury of living close to our extended family, yet desire and need their support. Dropping a line to let them know about a blood test result, the extra half mile we were able to walk, the thrill of completing chemotherapy, or the grieving we have gotten in touch with can be honestly and simply expressed without feeling pressured to say one word more than feels safe. The length of a letter is truly unimportant. As with every element of *Writing Your Way Through Cancer*, it's your own healing journey that takes precedence.

Unsent letters can be revelatory in our healing journey. Facing a life-threatening illness often catapults us into a world of memories. Some we cleave to, some we had hoped to forget. Healing may require us to dig into these past wounds in order to heal the present and thus release ourselves to the future. Sometimes it is unwise or impossible to clean up the past directly with someone. Unsent letters are a perfect tool in these situations. They are a safe, well-lit avenue we can walk down, without adding to our self-contained fears by making ourselves vulnerable to someone else's defenses or attacks.

Through unsent letters you can address the person directly, telling your story and how it felt to you. They are a quite handy tool for talking to the deceased, the excommunicated, the estranged. You can speak your own truth without comment. Again I must assert that some things need to be said directly. Unsent letters are not a substitute for nor shelter from relationship with all its ups and downs.

Letters, both sent and unsent, require us to listen. We must listen to what we have chosen to share with others, what has taken priority, the mood we wish to express. So often people remark, "Oh, I don't have time to write letters. It's so much easier to pick up the phone or e-mail." Yes, sometimes it is. I suggest that you go the extra distance.

Write your way through cancer on a piece of linen paper and send it to a loved one.

Don't let the greeting card company say it for you!

The Importance of Dreams

You don't have to be trained in Jungian psychology in order to learn from your dreams. One of my dearest friends who is trained in Jungian dreamwork recently told me that Jung said, "The dream never lies." For many years now I have kept a dream journal. Writing down my dreams lifted them out of the unconscious into the conscious world where I could then use them to listen to my inner voice and hone insight. My dreams have taught me a great deal about myself through windows I might have never peered into in my waking world. Over the years, as a direct result of writing down my dreams, I have been gifted with the evolving ability to work consciously in the dream, as well as to awaken myself in the midst of a dream in order to write down a particularly potent image. I ask for help *in* my dreams as well as *through* my dreams, and have grown to deeply trust their communication.

The best time to write down a dream is the moment you wake up. Everyone has experienced the frustration of trying to remember dream imagery that is rapidly slipping back into the unconscious. I recommend keeping a notepad by the bed. If you awaken in the night from a dream you want to recall, but wish not to fully wake up, turn on a flashlight and jot down key words. Make writing the dream in full a priority in the morning. Remember, the farther away we get from the dream the foggier it usually becomes.

How much you choose to *analyze* your dreams is up to you. Sometimes the imagery couldn't be any clearer—nor the lesson. Sometimes the imagery is very strong, intense, even frightening. While it's all familiar in the dream world, it may be confusing or surrealistic in the waking world. Through your writing try asking the characters, images, even structures in your dreams—such as carnival rides, submarines or escalators—what they wish to say.

Please keep in mind that "nightmares" also have something valuable to communicate. One of the principles I have practiced with my daughter is not using the label "nightmare" when referring to her dreams. Having "suffered" from strong dreams as a child, which became nightmares due to lack of guidance, I have been determined to offer my child a more enlightened relationship to her dreams.

A simple principle to follow when working with your dreams: all the players are parts of you. The demons and angels, doctors and nurses, charlatans and priests, cobras and kittens are all symbolic of the multi-dimensional you. Accepting, integrating and listening to this symphony of voices can awaken thrilling introspection.

Some dreams are literal, some prophetic. Writing them can help you learn to make these distinctions, as well as a host of others. You may wish to include your dreams in your cancer journal rather than a separate dream journal, or record them in both. I refer to the dreams I am sharing here over and over again. They help me in both the dark times as well as the light.

From My Journal

April 1998
pre-surgery

Each day lately I wake up singing. Today I just couldn't not be happy. Something about facing one's fears brings joy.

Dream: I am walking down an alleyway. Don't recall where I am going or why. A strange man begins walking beside me and starts to harass me. He reaches over and grabs my breast, pulling at my clothes.

At first I am frightened and begin to run. He chases after me, continuing to pick at my clothes and bother me. Suddenly I become conscious in the dream and hear my spiritual guide instruct, "Don't run. Turn and face your fear!" I immediately stop in my tracks, turn to the man, look him very straight in the eye and speak with absolute intention and attention, "You don't scare me. I'm not afraid of you. Not one bit! Now get the hell out of here. Leave me alone. You can't do anything to me. Do you hear me? I'm not in the least bit afraid of you." I stare straight into his eyes with not so much as a blink.

He turns to run away. I shout out to him, "You think you can get away, but you can't! Watch this." I turn to a man who has mysteriously and almost instantaneously materialized. I know he is a guide sent to aid me in my dream. The man has a very large strawberry birthmark on his face. I turn to him, point to the molester who is still in seeing and hearing range, and shout out so that he can hear, "See that man. He tried to rape me. Get him!"

I immediately woke up, ecstatic, knowing it was about the cancer.

May, 1999

Dream:

I am at home alone in a house in the neighborhood I grew up in. This house is white and very elegantly appointed—very zen, almost empty. Suddenly I hear someone trying to open the door. Immediately I know this someone is trying to break into the house. I feel fear rise up. Through a window across a hallway I see a strange man looking in. He is white, and not overly scary, but definitely "the enemy."

Our eyes meet, but only for an instant; and I take off! The layout of this house is unfamiliar so it is like running a maze. Nevertheless as I make it outside I can hear him walking through the house in pursuit of me. He is clearly not a burglar. He is after me! I run for my life down the street. And man-o-man can I run. Just like when I was a kid— FAST; FAST; FAST. I get clean away and don't look back till I am way down the street, winded and victorious.

Then in the dream though my heart was pounding and fear was still roaming around, the inner witness [me] says to the runner [me], "That man was cancer—and you got away! Yipee!!!"

Dumping

My definition of dumping includes ranting, complaining, whining, spewing or verbal discharging. It is not a form of writing I can whole-heartedly support. Dumping our anger, resentment, bitterness, jealousy, victimization on paper is not much different from bitching to a friend, health care person or loved one. Contrary to the way it "feels" in the moment, dumping is characteristically fighting our feelings or disguising them under the costume of drama and exaggeration. Venting takes us on a joyride through the emotions. On the other hand, writing through our feelings allows us to consider the scenery along the way, as well as cruise at our own speed, and rest when we need to. There's space to integrate, reflect, explore.

Conscious discharging of emotional energy may be called for randomly throughout our healing. The keyword here is *conscious.* We can take to the woods, or beat a pillow, or ask a friend to bear witness to a venting session. Thus we implement the intention to purify and release a build-up of negativity. We self-check by making note of any insight or revelation that manages to surface out of the "waste" so that we can return to this potential gem later in our writing.

Unmonitored dumping is self-indulgent, and my experience is that it can actually hinder healing from within. Dumping carries with it the risk of reinforcing the very attitudes that may have contributed to a compromised immune system to begin with.

The obvious question in *Writing Your Way Through Cancer* is how to tell the difference between dumping and expressing real feelings. The quickest most reliable feedback mechanism I have found is to assess how I feel after writing. If I am drained, overwhelmed, anxious, obsessed, then I most likely have been on a joyride. However, expressing, investigating and accepting the truth of our feelings will *ultimately* leave us feeling whole, even if it takes awhile to arrive there. Encountering repressed anger, bottled up tears, or wounds that are not ready for the bandage to come off is part and parcel to the process of writing. Most likely we will not experience closure at the end of every writing period.

If you find yourself "at the dump":

• Take a break. Take a walk. Meditate. Steam in a hot bath.

See if respite creates a space to move past the desire to dump and into the feelings that may be buried underneath the garbage.

• Write the "dump," then write the situation just as it is. Try to use "I" statements.

Example: Dumping—"I hate, hate, hate getting CT scans. I'm sick of it!!! Why me?"

What is—"It's another CT scan day. Yuck. Barium, IV, etc. I'm angry, testy, hungry. Ice cream sounds good. I would rather go to a movie for the afternoon. Zone out. I know that zoning out is an escape. In this moment I am very clear that this CT is something that is 'necessary' *and* something I wish to escape. I can't escape it. I can't escape cancer. That makes me feel trapped."

Follow Your Heart

Immediately following my cancer surgery I embarked on an in-depth exploration of health and healing resources. I was determined to be an active participant in my treatment, however the ocean of cancer looked ominous and I knew I needed help in making informed choices. I read everything from articles in medical journals to simple recovery stories. I dove into oncological evaluations of Dukes III colon cancer while simultaneously viewing introductory videos from alternative healing clinics in Mexico. I listened to Carolyn Myss audio tapes and consulted Andrew Weil.

Through my investigation I learned a lot about the nature of cancer. I also learned something about the nature of authority and my relationship to it. Most of these resources provided profound help, especially in the beginning stages of recovery. The encouragement, camaraderie and confrontation encountered in these various materials helped me feel that the ocean could be navigated. Others had gone before me.

However, as I began to settle into life with cancer the need to listen less to the cancer authorities and more to myself steadily grew. At this stage it seemed that the more I read, the more discouraged I felt.

As my personal need lessened, I often heard strong and sometimes rigid opinions from others about the attitudes of cancer patients and the how's and why's of whether we recover or not. Especially after metastatic growth it was all too easy for me to dip into an unhealthy level of self-doubt and confusion instigated by these all-knowing authorities who, for the most part, had not actually *had* cancer. Too often I felt guilt because I hadn't been able to cure myself.

Fortunately, I had my writing as a means to honor my own story, explore my own feelings, refine my listening to my inner voice, and relax into some semblance of peace. One of the messages I heard was that I needed to take a break from reading about cancer and *live* my life.

Writing Your Way Through Cancer requires courage. Staying true to oneself is not always an easy process. Most of us have little modeling for listening to the heart, and the tendency to seek external validation is pressing in the New-Age cancer healing community. Yet, I have found that the more closely I listen to my own heart, the better I feel—physically, emotionally and spiritually. The more I honor my own sense of what will contribute to my healing and transformation, the more permission my inner wisdom or authentic voice has to speak to me.

At one point during a healing crisis I went through while visiting friends in Europe I called my doctor from overseas. Of course, there wasn't much she could do across continents other than offer some consultation and answer technical questions, but it was reassuring to speak to her. At the end of the conversation she astutely asked, "Are you writing?" "Yes," I answered. "Good," she replied. "It's your most important medicine."

Listening to the heart is a very personal affair. Whether your heart is inspired to speak when you stand on a grassy knoll, kneel in a cathedral, listen to Rachmaninoff or write poetry, listening to and following your heart will carry you more strongly and compassionately across the ocean of cancer to the shores of healing.

From My Journal

August 1999

The last few days "my" writing has been bringing up a lot about writing itself. The way I can best describe it is wishing to rest in a context wherein writing is greater than self-absorption and self-reference. Suddenly I was disturbingly aware of how even when I'm "writing about the domain of the miraculous," it's still "me" writing "my" experience or "my" observations or "my" opinion, "my" limitations, "my" revelry, "my" practice, "my" realization, "my" lessons. Yesterday this observation was so dramatic that I literally felt as though I could not bear to spend one more second "listening" to myself in my mind as I wrote.

Let It Write You

I wrote a poem a few days ago that began with the image of a hootchie-kootchie man and ended up describing an algae-sucker in an aquarium. Huh? In poetry, the shortest distance between two points may not always be a straight line. The algae sucker wanted to be heard so it shouted a little louder than the hootchie-kootchie man. I let my pen follow the trail of the sucker, knowing I could go back to the hootchie-kootchie man some other time. (Gnarly ole guys like him are used to waiting.)

When we give license to our heart it can and will drive us into realms of feelings, perceptions, discoveries that we might never have traveled into any other way. It will speak, sometimes faintly, but it will speak. Encourage yourself to listen.

A diagnosis of cancer has provoked me into taking more risks. I travel off the paved road with less anxiety about who's driving and where the road is going than previously. I also encounter my habitual fear, but the awakening to the challenge of living life to the fullest in every moment is a reliable guide.

Writing Your Way Through Cancer is an invitation to try the circuitous route and discover where it leads you. There are times when it feels important to stay focused. Maintaining focus and *letting it write you* are not contradictions. The greater context for both has to do with giving up unhealthy control and releasing into a deeper level of trust, which will in turn enhance healing.

Ikebana

IV infiltration at midnight
Bruised veins
Blood pressure cuff
    squeezing arm at 3 AM
Doctor's rounds at 6:30
Sneeze at 8 that
    rips into incision
        like a blow torch
Tears ooze from eyes
A pot of homegrown iris
delivered at noon
Exquisite sunshine yellow
        pale lavender
Their sweet lovely fragrance
    enveloping hospital smell

Each day
I walk the floor
IV pole in tow
Past
    nurses filling out charts
        dispensing pills
            saving lives
Past
    rooms with game shows blaring
        old men on oxygen
            pale white wrinkled bottoms
                hanging out of hospital gowns
Past
    loneliness
        and
            suffering

To return to
Monet's Garden
To clear table
    of Kleenex, unread magazines, wilted compresses
To practice
Ikebana
Aware of breath
    empty mind
        balance of yin and yang

Pain vanishes at this altar
Cancer   becomes
Nothing
   more
      than
         cancer
Torturous NG tube
   threaded through nostrils
      down throat
         into stomach
Transforms
Into fading edges
   of a bad dream

For a moment
All existence is

Just iris

Nurses from all around
Stop by
Knocking softly
Sheepishly asking
   Can I see the flowers
      we heard of them
         down in x-ray
           up in OB

Beauty is hard to find
In the mire of illness
The stench of death
Besides
I was happy to have
Nurses
Come to view
Ikebana
Instead of
Cancer

Part II

Writing Through the Stages
Stage 1. Coping With Cancer

From My Journal

February 1999

I noticed how tired I was. I stopped for a moment, looked at myself in the mirror and asked, "Why are you 'pushing'?" I could see the aura of that driven mode like a halo around me. Over the years I have been forced to slow down so much, to pay attention to my workaholic pattern. Now luckily I catch it pretty quickly. So I was aware of that first inkling of "racing."

The reflection in the mirror gave me my answer. I was building a belief system that if I can keep up with everyone else, move at the pace of modern Western civilization (which incidentally means work till ya drop) then I must be cancer-free. This is a fairly subtle almost subconscious belief system. Parallel to this aspect of the inner game is the belief that if I am tired by 7:30 P.M., achy, needing to miss my walk for even one day for any reason, especially any physical reason, resistant to taking my twentieth vitamin, etc., then it might mean there's an opening somewhere for "IT" to return.

I was also aware that in the subtler realms as well I was being haunted a bit by old symptoms. That if any signs of symptoms I had prior to surgery managed to show up then the entity could/can/would/and will use that to induce fear of recurrence. So I looked at myself a while longer reaching inside for tenderness, compassion, and "mother" and reminded myself that rest is very important; but more importantly, that "I" don't have to prove anything to "myself." That "I" don't have to be able to drink everyone else under the table. That it's a common scenario for cancer patients to fall into—a classic defense and understandable, but unnecessary.

Living life to the fullest in every moment is not about racing in the Indy 500 seven days a week. Living life in the fullest is about quality, breath, simplicity and feeling. So on we go.

Shock

No one truly ever expects to be diagnosed with cancer. Yet fear of cancer is instilled in many of us from an early age. We are inundated with statistics, TV ads, and special news reports which graphically depict the horrendous number of women who die from breast cancer each year or the even greater number of lung cancer "victims." Magazine illustrations warn us of the regiments of carcinogens that are in reality impossible to avoid yet capable of generating intense paranoia. Most everyone has experienced some form of loss resulting from cancer. Many of us have witnessed a loved one's battle, while holding a hand as they slipped away. As a result, we may grow up cultivating a fear of cancer which ultimately does nothing to prepare us for the shock of reality.

In spite of how informed we may feel, a diagnosis of cancer is always a shock. I have shared with many friends my own experience, simply put, that life irrevocably changes once you have been diagnosed with cancer. In moments of feeling totally alone with my fear, grief, anger and determination I have on occasion heard myself respond to someone's attempts at consolation, "No, actually you don't know exactly how I feel. And quite frankly I don't need you to. I just ask you to consider that life is what it is on one side of the line and it changes completely once you cross over." The crossing over is not a choice. However, how we handle or cope with being on the other side is.

Shock is a psycho-physical state that affords some unusual opportunities. Our usual guards are stripped away, leaving us vulnerable and open. It can be a time in which caution is necessary due to this heightened vulnerability. However, because it is an altered state, we may also experience a clarity that is not normally available. Testimonies and accounts of extraordinary experiences, insights, visions and superhuman feats are often reported during a state of shock.

Writing promises tremendous value at this time. The simple act of externalizing the myriad of feelings that are triggered with the impact of a diagnosis of cancer can bring insight and objectivity to a situation that typically feels totally overwhelming. Writing can help orient us to the strength of our own wisdom. Shock is often accompanied by a sense of being lost and out-of-control. *Writing Your Way Through Cancer* can literally function as a grounding rod. It can lift us out of the trenches of fear, confusion, denial and victimization into the fields of our spirituality and higher consideration. Time and again my writing has taken me from self-reference, self-pity, complaint and pain into self-discovery and revelation. I am able to answer my own questions, make my own decisions, because through writing I have chosen to listen.

The shock of diagnosis is usually coupled with the question of treatment. Typically before the cancer patient has time to even begin digesting the news, questions about the future begin. Luckily my surgeon *asked* if I wished to consider chemotherapy and radiation. He kindly and very patiently explained all he knew about the program that would most likely be prescribed. He *listened* to my battery of questions and answered the ones he could, admitting honestly to the ones he couldn't. He *encouraged* me to talk with my naturopath, whom he had bravely invited to my surgery. I was lucky—immensely lucky. This is a rare scenario. My part was to expect/demand that my healing program include "me."

It is my observation that the majority of newly diagnosed cancer patients have a slightly, if not profoundly, different experience. The scenario is one where they are *not asked* but rather *told* what the treatment will be. A patient still reverberating from the shock waves often finds themselves dazed and shaky. Consequently, they are willing to follow along and perhaps agree with any proposal for "survival" offered. I have both read accounts of and spoken to cancer patients who confessed that they never felt they had the time nor the personal power to really think through their treatment plan, consider options and thus make informed choices.

My father, who died from an undetermined cancer, stated quite frankly, just weeks before his death, that he knew chemotherapy could not save his life. He confessed that he had really only undergone the treatment to please his doctors. He said, "Dr. Jones believes so strongly in this. I'm filled with cancer. What does it matter to me? If it's going to give him some comfort, then why not let him feel good?"

Writing Your Way Through Cancer can shine light on attitudes such as these. Had my father truly been in charge of his own healing, perhaps he would have chosen to return home and spend his final days in an environment that supported conscious transition rather than succumb to the violent side effects he endured from chemotherapy.

Many of us will have already made treatment choices and be well on our way before deciding to engage in a writing practice. However, shock can come at any time. I was in a deeper state of shock with news of metastatic lung lesions than I was with my initial diagnosis. At that time writing was indeed the stable ground upon which I could stand, reflect, ask my body and my soul about the next step, as well as listen to the truth being spoken from the heart. I was able to tune in to my own inner wisdom. I could write through my feelings of betrayal, anger and fear, into integration and clarity. Remember, *Writing Your Way Through Cancer* is not a technique for avoiding feeling, but rather a well-lit path into the rich and revelatory regions of the self. Shock is one "inn" along the road.

From My Journal

January 1999
San Francisco

I arrived here safely after a very long day. The nurse called Tuesday morning and said, "I'll just read the CT scan results to you so that it's all clear." It went something like this: "There are three nodules on the right lung, two on the left. The evidence shows metastatic lung carcinoma, etc." Then the nurse proceeded to explain that the nodules are presently too small for even a needle biopsy. I was in shock. I really did not believe there was any more cancer in my body. And to be quite honest, I have moments in which I don't even believe there is now. Sounds kinda crazy, huh, but when I feel into my body right now, in this moment, it feels so open, clear, healthy.

Anyway, for the rest of the day I found myself in a deep, deep state of shock which emptied into immense grieving, then into waves of fear, even panic, states of confusion and all this contraction, if you will, being somewhat held in a net of profound gratitude, crystal clear clarity and a rarefied atmosphere of love for God. Though I could not bear to be alone externally, I was profoundly aware of how alone I was inside, regardless of how many people were supporting me on the outside.

The Other Shoe

The other shoe
    dropped
Hit
    b
      o
        t
          t
            o
              m
With a silent
CRASH
Causing reverberations
In the inner ear
That rippled
    outward in concentric
Circles of
Grief and fear
Whose centers were
Radiant with
    utter tranquillity

Circles
Spots on lungs
    too small for needle biopsy
Round cells
    with nuclei
Shapes of eternal recurrence
The cycle of
            Birth
    and   and
    Death   Death
    and   and
    Rebirth   Rebirth
        and   and
            Death

Fear cycles into faith
Despair circles into hope
Grief comes round to gratitude
The sound of the
    other shoe dropping

Echoes
Through the soul
Singing
When you live, just live
    When you die, just die

Treatment

Depending on the treatment or combination of treatments you may choose, the process of cancer treatment is one requiring patience, courage and endurance. Every treatment or regime from chemotherapy to green tea requires stamina and consistency. The first step after diagnosis in the process of healing is answering the question, "What next?" Depending on the type and stage of your cancer the answer may be simple and obvious, or complicated and confusing.

My own situation was not so simple. Surgery was indeed the most obvious option, and although I was not excited over the prospect of an invasive procedure, I was thankful for the possibility of emancipating the body from the immense stress it was under. Prior to surgery I knew very little about cancer. I knew even less about treatment. I had watched my father suffer the ravages of chemotherapy, which could not have possibly helped him. His cancer was much too advanced. I was familiar with many forms of alternative healing, having prescribed to an array of them over the years. What I did know without question was that I needed to be in charge of my own healing. I had not felt victimized by cancer and I refused to feel victimized by my treatment. Therefore, an informed choice was crucial. Though I had my opinion about chemotherapy I knew it was essential for me to hear the facts before I made my decisions.

Writing afforded me tremendous clarity and self-empowerment. It helped me wade through the fear, anger, grief and overwhelm that hovered over me as I tried to recover and heal from major surgery. It's not uncommon for medical professionals, both traditional and alternative, to communicate an intense sense of urgency around beginning treatment. This urgency is not necessarily unfounded. However, it encourages the patient to begin their cancer healing from a context of scarcity of time. Scarcity does not contribute much to the mood of healing. Writing is a tool that helps to bend or stretch time. You may indeed not have the luxury of a lot of time to research a particular treatment or visit an unusual clinic. However, you can demand the time, even if only twenty-four hours, to get clear with yourself regarding your body and your decisions for treatment.

I chose to share my cancer diagnosis with only my closest friends and relatives. It was imperative in my healing for me to have ample psychic space to be able to give adequate attention to my physical body *mending*, my emotional body *feeling* and my spiritual body *communicating*. I knew my attention would be compromised if I had to tell my story, explain my potential choices, and most of all defend myself against others' negative thoughts and projections. "The less said the better," was my experience. Yours may be different.

Remember, no one else can do your treatment. It's your body, your time, your money. You need to believe in your choices, and all choices have their pluses and minuses. *Writing Your Way Through Cancer* will help you stay in touch with your treatment's effectiveness over time, empowering you to listen for any adjustments you may wish to make, as well as persevere through the times that are difficult.

Here are a few exercises that could help clarify your own intuitive feelings.

1. Refer back to the essay *Dialogues* on page 24. Write a dialogue with yourself or someone else about your treatment choices. For example, dialogue with:

- Your mother
- Your partner or spouse
- Your oncologist
- Your priest, minister or rabbi

- Your family doctor
- Your adult son or daughter
- Your close friend
- Your counselor, therapist

Read back thoughtfully over what you have written and notice where or how you might be:

- Defending
- Reacting
- Adapting
- Denying

- Rebelling
- Compromising
- Feeling or acting "paralyzed"

2. List each treatment option:

Treatment	Pros	Cons	My Concerns

This detailed list could provide questions for your next doctor's visit, counseling session, or cancer support group meeting.

The Decision

I went out into the woods
Grandfather tree
Waited
I laid my palm
    against the truth
        carved into his bark
Dug my bare toes
    deep into the mulch
        around his tremendous trunk
Let his branches
    tangle in my hair
So that he had me
    wrapped up in him
        papoosed
Safely bound to the earth
Ready to stand
Like a warrior
In the face of grief

Grandfather tree
Held me close
Close enough
To breathe his ancient wisdom
    into my soul
Close enough
To whisper through the breeze
    that caressed the leaves
        in my hair
That a cure is not the point
That death
Is just the beginning
He rocked me
    in his swaying branches
So tenderly
That I could feel
Life
Pulsing through my cells

Then Grandfather tree
    parted the bark
        at the center of his
            holy trunk
Saying "Look child"
There was a window
"Look inside" he commanded
Through this magical portal
I saw
The seven days of creation
The heavens
    oceans
        mesas
            canyons
The deer
    mouse
        goldfinch
          hare
I watched
I knew
Then the window vanished
Grandfather tree bent
    his magnificent head low
And kissed my temple
One last time

    Go now
    He whispered
    Walk with strength
    Face your life
        and your death
    With open eyes
    With grateful heart
    With trusting soul

From My Journal

August 1998

I've noticed as the initial healing from the surgery becomes more complete how different my body feels, how many things are changed. For example, I can feel my bodily fluids actually flowing more freely. My blood feels thicker, richer, happier. My lymph fluids feel light and clear, moving easefully. I actually feel there is more water in my skin, my hair, my nails. Everything, quite simply put, feels more liquid.

Another area in which I have noticed a tacit difference is in my dreams. My dreams seem more available to me and a lot clearer. In fact, my whole sleeping pattern is lighter, less constricted, and certainly there is less scarcity around sleep.

It's enlivening and magical to be in touch with the physical body at this level. To be able to feel down into the veins, vessels, and arteries, to touch the blood—to perceive its composition, its density, its smoothness, its raw power. Blood is a powerful fluid. Much of this sheer awakening to the complexity and simplicity of the bodily fluids I attribute to a kind of cellular transformation that is taking place. I guess a very compact way of describing this internal awareness is to say my inner state is one of Joy. The organs, the tissues, the bones, the cells, the atoms, the blood, the lymph are brightening to a state of Joy.

Pain

"Are you in pain?" my friend asked after hearing that the intense heal-ing work I had been doing over the past year was due to cancer.

"Yes," I calmly answered. "I am in pain, but it's not what you most likely think."

Some forms of cancer are relatively painless, particularly in the early stages. Others, such as bone cancer, are apparently excruciating. Whichever the case, most of us will encounter some degree of pain in our healing. Physical pain, emotional pain, psychic pain and spiritual pain are just a few of the myriad shades and colors of pain. Sometimes treatment can be more painful than the cancer itself. In fact, whether we have cancer or not, pain is an unavoidable fact of life.

I like to think of pain as a teacher, which seems almost impossible sometimes. We expect our teachers to be wise, gentle and compas-sionate. Nonetheless, pain has a unique gift to offer us—pain is able to reflect to us very directly, a great deal about ourselves. It can quickly reveal our desperation for attention or our blatant refusal to accept nurturing. It often shines a light on childhood memories associated with pain and how we were cared for or neglected. It can offer insight into a quality of tenacity or courage we never knew we had. It can cat-apult us into the conflict of making choices about using narcotics, being desensitized, feeling out of control, or reaching for some relief so that we can treasure our fleeting moments with our family, children, grandkids. All of these situations contain a life lesson.

Pain produces vulnerability. Some of us hope and pray to never have to *feel* the level of pain cancer can cause. Others pray to never have to choose between excruciating physical pain and ending our life in a morphine induced sleep. A distinction I try to make in my own work with pain is between pain and suffering. The two are common-ly paired without much thought. I have experienced pain with suffer-ing and pain without suffering. I have also experienced suffering that is a result of my *resistance* to feeling the pain. Resistance creates ten-sion (which is one of its organic functions). It can also give rise to suf-fering.

Relaxing into our pain sounds like a contradiction to say the least. However, through the use of breath, visualization and massage, I have been able at times to cease the frantic search for pain relief. A few days after my cancer surgery I was able to manage my pain with only Extra Strength Tylenol™. This was a definite challenge for the nurses, sim-ply because they are trained to assist patients in numbing their pain.

Writing Your Way Through Cancer is a perfect canvas for pain to paint its lessons upon. Let your pain splatter like Jackson Pollock, dis-tort like Picasso, thunder like El Greco, soften like Monet. You may find that if you can open up to your pain the wisdom it speaks will take you deep into the far reaches of your soul.

Remember—heroism is not the point. Pain as Teacher is a tangent point for *Writing Your Way Through Cancer.*

Needles, Blood, Vampires

Needles come at me
Like vampires
The smell of blood
    filling their nostrils
The desire for salt on their lips
    propelling their wings
Needles
Biting into the flesh
Leaving blue black bruises
    up and down my arms
        in the backs of my hands
            bracelets around my wrists

I watch vials of blood
    come out
Bags of medicine go in
I look at needles
    taped to arms
I think about
The blood
Veins give so freely
Precious blood
The Blood of the Lamb
The Blood of Christ
Sacrificial Blood
Blood on the Altar
    in the Tabernacle
The blood of slaves
       crusaders
       children with leukemia
I think about the blood
That flows
    between a woman's legs
After giving birth
I offer a prayer
    of thanks
To veins
That surrender to

Needle and nurse
Vampire and rabbi

Today I imagine blood
Free
Of pirates who use these
    sacred blue waters
To transport
Contraband cancer cells
    into the lymph
        the tissue
I visualize white cells
    in nifty little motorboats
        Greenpeace plastered on the side
Zipping over white caps
Cleaning up polluted waters
Seizing smugglers, poachers
Murderers
Saving innocent lives

I caress my veins
    with my mind
Stroke them with tender thoughts
Thank them for
Their sacrifice
This mother aches
    to promise
Her tired and frightened
    children
That this time
    will be the last time
But this mother
    is no common liar
So she coaxes them
    with sweet words
To come out of hiding
For just a little while
To open up the locks
And let the medicine flow
    into their channels
And mix with the river
    of Holy Blood

I beg them
To lift the barricades and
Bring the Red Cross rations
        to the army of white cells
So they can
March into Hell
For this somewhat
Holy cause

Denial

Denial appears to be a traveling companion of cancer. Whether denial affords us the luxury of believing we have more time to think things over, get our life in order so that we can then deal with cancer, or keep our dreams and hopes for the future intact, it must be transformed if true healing is to ever take place. Denial is one of those players who can easefully wear many different hats—from the helmet of a warrior, to the crown of thorns of a martyr, to the beatific halo of a saint. I have caught myself numerous times brandishing my sword and shield in order to fight what we have come to label "our battle with cancer," only to come crashing down feeling hopeless defeat at the news of a not-so-happy x-ray result. Denial has a reputation for being synonymous with pretense or burying our head in the sand. However, I see those as only one manifestation of denial.

The distinction I am learning to make in relationship to denial is the difference between denial and acceptance. A very wise spiritual teacher counseled me to practice accepting that *reality is reality*. When I can accept *what is*, I increase my healing potential exponentially. A positive attitude then includes a range of feelings, all of which are part of me. I don't have to judge my emotions as good or bad. I don't have to try and fit into some preconceived picture of a perfect cancer patient. One of the ways I can spot denial is that it does not embrace change. The two are at odds. Acceptance may choke a bit on the first sip of change, but a mood of acceptance will eventually accept change into its flow. Change is part of growing and learning, even when the perceived eventuality may not be the "happy ending" we had hoped for.

Denial suppresses not only a host of emotions, it also keeps a lid on living. *Writing Your Way Through Cancer* can be a great stalker against the wily ways of denial—mainly because our journal page is a safe place to be who we are, express both our fears and revelations, and move out of the contracted position of denial into the expanded domain of acceptance.

Remember: Denial often shows up as an inner voice that tries desperately to squelch all other voices. Let your writing be a listener to the whole of you.

From My Journal
July 1999
France

It seems important in the process of healing to be able to gently rest in the gift of strength without slipping into the illusion of being immortal. It's occurred to me that our attachment to the idea of immortality—which we see as giving us expansiveness, eternal existence and so forth—is actually a form of limitation. Conversely, accepting our true mortality is what frees us to explore the idea of untold universes which exist far beyond our wildest dreams. When I am able to face the truth of my mortality I am aware of still having to encounter habitual notions of fear of death, uncertainty of the unknown, sentimental attachments and a broad spectrum of human limitations. However, I am also able to intuit "the beyond," which is a bit like experimenting with the focusing lens in a camera. I am able to bring the foreground into focus while simultaneously blurring the background, and vice versa. I guess it's a bit like being at the effect of the smaller picture, but being able to still see the bigger picture.

The illusion of immortality not only creates limitation in the field of looking at death with the vision of possibility, it also (and perhaps more importantly) cramps the scope of being able to live life to the fullest in every moment. Limited thinking fosters limited thinking. Limited thinking inhibits invention and creativity. Limited thinking promotes scarcity, insecurity, even despair. Limited thinking ambushes possibility and the gesture to change or transform with permanence.

Ode to Hitler . . . and Cancer

She said   I turn 60 tomorrow
I said   So you were alive
        during World War II
Her head dropped
Cheeks flushed
Ashamed
She whispered   yes

She was only seven
When Hitler marched across
    her soul

And the sins of the fathers
    and mothers...

Poor sixty-year-old-seven-year-old girl
It wasn't enough for her
To live on potatoes
For four years
To know hunger and fear
And hatred
To know
    (as only a seven-year-old's heart can know)
That something was
Very very wrong

It was a mortal sin
To speak of it
To whisper to anyone
Even God
That her father
Was a Nazi

Don't speak about it
EVER
And maybe
    just maybe
It will vanish
Into thin air
Like six million Jews

Most everyone
I know
Feels the same way
About cancer
Don't speak about
IT
And maybe
    just maybe
It will go away

Anger

During recovery from my cancer surgery I discovered while still in the hospital that my veins were not only traumatized from repeated infiltrations, they were elusive, delicate and "uncooperative." Prior to my surgery I had not been aware of this difficulty. However, as time went on, this condition showed no signs of changing. At a follow-up CT scan the technician and an assistant attempted entering the veins at six different sites before an IV therapist and nursing supervisor were able to successfully start an IV at the seventh try. Needless to say I was in tears, shivering (from both the trauma and the 65° temperature controlled room), bruised and frustrated.

Before the seventh attempt, the nurse asked if I wanted them to stop trying, informing me I would have to sign a form which would actually state to my doctor that "I refused to cooperate." *Refused to cooperate... Excuse me...* They enlightened me that it was the only explanation on the form. Through my tears and pain after an hour of being "stuck," I gritted my teeth and said, "Just get a vein! I refuse to leave here until this procedure is complete. I've invested too much time, energy and patience to walk away having my efforts bureaucratically labeled as uncooperative. Please ignore the tears and proceed." Besides, I had no intention of returning to do it all again.

I was angry. Not because they couldn't get a vein, per se. I was angry at their refusal to call in an expert earlier—which my nurse friend later informed me was a breach of protocol. They were determined to be heroes, refusing to admit defeat. I was angry at the system's loopholes. I was especially angry at the all-too-common policy of blaming the patient when the responsibility is obviously the health care professional's. I was angry at having another invasive procedure. I was angry about having cancer. Period.

Anger is just another emotion, like sadness, joy, fear, delight. However, it tends to be the one that gets a lot of attention. In its raw form, anger, like all emotions, is healthy. It's a natural response to any number of situations. Repressed anger is not so healthy. Few of us were raised in an environment in which healthy anger was modeled. Many of us witnessed or were the recipients of unhealthy anger or deeply repressed anger, which was unpredictable and usually unowned. Often, as a result, we either incorrectly claimed the anger as ours, assumed we were the cause, or unconsciously decided to express our anger in the same ways.

A diagnosis of cancer commonly triggers indignation, anger, even rage. We may feel betrayed and at the effect of having our life interrupted, perhaps gravely. Many of the choices we are faced with certainly do not feel like choices. Suddenly our life no longer seems to be our own. It's okay to be angry about this unwelcomed and especially uninvited insinuation. The challenge with anger is how to express it healthily and move on. Attachment to our anger is just as "cancering" as attachment to our fear of death.

Writing has been a savior for me in learning how to confront, befriend, express, and ultimately transform my anger. One of the clearest revelations I have had since diagnosis is that, at the risk of possibly both alienating and making others pay, I have discovered that all my life I have been ashamed of my anger. Although inroads have been made over the years through therapy, yoga and many years of serious meditation, nothing has shed light on the truth of healthy anger as brilliantly as cancer. And oh what a relief it has been to find permission to be angry at a situation I have every right to feel angry about! Through writing I have been learning to listen to the anger and express it without dumping on or blaming my loved ones for a situation they cannot change. I am also learning how much anger likes to dramatize and be romanced.

In writing my way through cancer I tend to express my anger through poetry. The form lends itself to strong words, exclamations, dramatic vows and poetic promise of transformation. One afternoon, as an Arizona monsoon blew up, I put on Carl Orff's *Carmina Burana* and through tears and strings of curse words I wrote a very long poem that began with rage and anger and ended in forgiveness and gratitude. It was not just the words on paper that had melted into softness. Deep healing had taken place inside of me.

Try writing your way through anger. Start a poem with a line that ignites this emotion for you. If you don't have one immediately available try one or more of the following:

- I'm furious . . .

- Stormclouds of rage brew inside . . .

- Get off my back . . .

Remember: All writing doesn't have to end on a happy note.

Rebuking the Devil

Drove around
Last night
Turned off the radio
Rolled up the windows
Blasted the heat
Intentional discomfort
Incinerator on wheels
I shouted
Like a madwoman
    on a street corner
       in the Bronx

       Get the Fuck
       Outta here
       You've had your fun
       Now
       Beat It
       Scram
       I've been patient
       Understanding
       Even compassionate at times
       And now
       I'm telling you to
       Clear out
       Now
       Today
       Vamoose
       Beat It
       Cancer
       Git
       All the way out
       And a little warning
       No setting up
       Your filthy little camp
       Somewhere else
       In
          My
             Body

Felt so good
Felt like a Texas preacher
'Buking the devil

Fear

What can I possibly say about fear that has not been said or you have not already experienced? Fear has been the most persistent obstacle facing me since diagnosis. It lurks around every corner and quite honestly has served me immensely.

Rather than write an essay on fear I feel the most honest thing for me to do is include a section of journal excerpts. Embracing reality as reality and continuing to make every gesture possible to relinquish the illusion of control are, for now, the only tools I have that allow me to greet my fear with some semblance of acceptance, remembering that fear is a great teacher.

From My Journal

July 1999

Just this moment my journal flipped open to the back which has a little explanation of the Persian writing on the front cover—the heading reads, "The war of the Sons of Light against the Sons of Darkness." That's exactly what these confrontations with the hungry ghosts who dwell in the land of fear feels like.

Part of what hangs me up is the expectation I have of being able to confront the Sons of Darkness without fear, walk through this hell-realm, this mine field and not be afraid. The strategy of perfectionism has fostered a ridiculous conclusion that a warrior doesn't "feel" afraid. At this moment I am remembering the flavor of Carlos Castenada's journeys into the underworld and how much fear he encountered. I'm not so sure it's a matter of "making friends with fear," and all that stuff, as much as just being with the "nature of fear": The "what is" of fear.

It's clear to me that God is definitely trying to teach me something about the essential nature of fear. Oh yes. Indeed. And the more I can drop my idea of how I think I'm supposed to respond, the quicker the true nature of It will be revealed.

From My Journal

August 1999

Fear has come knocking at my door again. I have had a respite from it for a while and now she has come to continue teaching me the lesson she has to offer. I certainly do not know the lesson of this lesson so am not able to consciously set my aim on anything tangible. I perceive it to be more complex than a simple intellectual guess or assumption that the lesson is trust or surrender, faith—the logical conclusions. Something I am learning through this process is that the Intelligence of the Divine cannot be second-guessed, is not limited to the domain of the intellect or the mind, and if left to its own brilliance will communicate exactly what we need for transformation to take place.

A few nights ago I was clearly having a chemical reaction to something in my IV. I was also plagued by predictable symptoms of anxiety— dry mouth, shaking to different degrees of intensity, hot flashes and mental confusion. Many months ago, when this phenomena was so strong— initiated by the discovery of the lung lesions—I received a clear inner communication to go into the fear alone. Though at times I felt abandoned in that, I knew I was being sent there for a reason, and, as I have written before I could not possibly know what awaited me on the other side. However, after going there alone over and over I was blessed on the other side with a visitation from Buddha, compassionately instructing me to take refuge in fear.

I have practiced taking refuge and it has brought me through many swamps of fear. However, I have been aware of the ego attachment to taking refuge as a means of eradicating fear. I'm quickly learning "It" doesn't work this way. At times I have even had the extraordinary experience of fear being nothing—nothing less, nothing more—than Fear. That's All. Just Fear. And, on an occasion or two, I have been gifted with the awesome though grotesquely uncomfortable experience of hanging out in Fear and being aware of the Ferocious face of God Himself.

The other night I reached out for the security of human comfort, which eased the fear somewhat. But, as usual, it was clear that no one can go there with me, or for me. No one can hold my hand on the other side. So I shook until I fell asleep hearing my last words before sleep being, "I'm not ready to die." The next morning when I awoke I felt the usual strung out feeling, but fear had crawled back into the shadows, and also, as usual, could not be called out.

A day of respite passed, then that night I was awakened out of a deep sleep to violent bodily shaking which ambushed me out of nowhere. I lay there for a while trying to will fear away; or better yet ignore her. No luck. I turned on the light, grabbed my pillow and planned to make a quick getaway. Fresh air . . . The porch. When I opened the door to go outside it seemed so dark out there. My body was shaking so intensely it was difficult to walk, but I managed to return for a flashlight.

As I stood in my room feeling the enveloping cloud of fear all around me I suddenly heard the inner voice tenderly speak into my ear. "This time go into it alone." I tried to resist, to turn a deaf ear, but I knew it would lead me into that place which always brings some form of salvation on the other side.

So I put my pillow back on the bed, gathered the cleaning supplies and went in to clean the bathroom. The fear did not totally vanish, but rather rose and fell like waves until the sea was calm. I cleaned for an hour or so—all the bathrooms, emptied trash. Then began to notice the body was integrated once again. I was ready to go to sleep.

Kali

Fear floats in
Draped in her hoary shroud
Toothless
Thirsty

I lay still
Hovering in the ethers somewhere
Between
Terror
    and
          adoration

Hypnotized
By her outstretched hand
Bony
Beckoning me

To come
Into her open arms
Nestle between her sagging breasts
Pillow my head
    upon her necklace of skulls
Take solace
She whispers

I rise
A somnambulist
Following
Into the nether regions
Not knowing
If I shall ever
Return

Stage 2. Living With Cancer

From My Journal

January 1999

What does it mean to Really Live? We speak of this so often but how many of us really know what it means to Live. To know without mere intellectual understanding that every passing second is death and rebirth.

A candle and incense burn before me. They each "die" a little every second, the wick becomes smaller, the ash longer. However, as the wick decreases the flame increases; as the ash lengthens the smoke becomes thicker. A pot of flowers stands between them. Gladiolas on a stalk continue to open as they bloom and die at the same time. Each day a new blossom opens at the top of the stalk as one wilts and dies at the bottom.

Time can only be lengthened or bent if we have our attention on the present moment. Grasping at the moment that has just passed will never buy us more time. Worry or anxiety over the next moment to come automatically puts us into the mood of fear and apprehension. All those states of attachment, grasping, holding on are states of contraction.

Acceptance is the state of expansion. Of course, the mind is not truly capable of even thinking or imagining that type of expansion, so even in "thinking" these thoughts the literal boundaries of my limited thinking are extremely narrow. In fact, as I write I am aware of experiencing a mental claustrophobia—trapped or shut-in by the limitations of the mind. It's as if I am longing to have my mind expand its vision and it cannot. At the same time I am also aware that straining and effort only create contraction rather than expansion.

From the time we are young children we hear the scientific theory that humans only use a tiny percentage of their brain; that the brain's capacity to cognize, invent, deduce, theorize, create is infinitely greater than "we" have even begun to touch. At this moment in time and space I am experiencing the absolute truth of this theory. I see that my opinions, ideas, notions, concepts, thoughts, discoveries, theories, realizations, satoris, free moments, understandings, beliefs are about as vast and far-reaching as my brother's pond compared to the area of all the oceans of the earth put together, and then some.

I'm actually experiencing the limitation of the mind in vivo. *I am also profoundly aware of the truth that there is no-thing "I" can do about it.*

Resilience

Resilience is a matter of perspective. I have always been a *do*-er. This quality has its positive side and its negative side. The positive: I get things done. The negative: I tend to define my self-worth by how much I *do*. Having met serious illness numerous times prior to cancer I have been given many opportunities to confront my *do*-ing-ness, attempting to balance it with *be*-ing. Simultaneous to plunging into this habitual way of approaching life I also began to see how critically I judged my journeys into illness as some fundamental weakness in character, poor attitude and a lack of resilience.

At one of my follow-up visits to the oncologist, my dear friend and advocate interrupted my report to the doctor, adjusting the facts, clarifying, proposing a reality check. When asked about my stamina, I had answered (habitually), "Well I feel I have compromised energy . . . blah, blah, blah." The correction, "Well, let's see. You got up at 5:30, wrote for an hour, showered, meditated, made juice, did your healing program, got your daughter up and ready for school, did a four-mile bike ride, worked on the book, did an IV, library trip, Aikido carpool, a brief nap and . . . all at forty-eight years of age with three surgeries in one and a half years. Hmmm . . . "

My body is tremendously resilient. It's amazing. It's forgiving. There's a very strong temptation for cancer patients to judge the immune system as weak or lacking resilience due to the mere fact that they have cancerous cells. A different perspective, one my own healing is steering me toward, is that my body is surviving cancer, multiple surgeries, repeated exposure to radiation, a host of other invasive procedures, not to mention pain. It bounces back time and again from doctor's fatalistic comments, neighbor's unconscious projections and many other cancer related stresses encountered here and there.

Writing Your Way Through Cancer can support the body maintaining its natural state of buoyancy. On days when you feel particularly heavy or burdened, try writing some haiku. Do a reality check like the one mentioned above. Reinforce resilience by appreciating the body's gracious acceptance of your particular treatment. Write about how quickly you recovered from a "set back." Congratulate, applaud, give thanks. Remember, just being able to write at all sometimes is a testimony itself to resilience.

From My Journal

June 1999

The body is indeed inspiring in its willingness to accept these invasions, to offer hospitality to this catheter in my chest—this foreign object that is plastic, high-tech, both masculine and feminine. Masculine in its plasticity and symbolism of the technology of this culture. Masculine in its representation of modern man's desire to increase longevity, beat the odds, and always win the game. Feminine in its flexibility, receptivity, willingness to bend to the grain of the muscle, the flow of the tissue. Feminine in its gesture to serve the human body by being a link between the heart and its erstwhile extensions, the veins, and by being an open channel through which both blood (the feminine) and medicine (the masculine) can flow as one, maintaining health, life, supporting the whole.

I can literally feel the tissue stretching to receive and accept. It's not a feeling of strenuous stretching necessarily, but indeed the body is on alert, guarded as it focuses attention on this new relationship.

I use the tool of visualization to assist the body with the mind. I see the catheter integrated, smoothly, easefully. I thank the veins in my arms and hands for their endurance over the past months. Each time (twice now) that I have received an infusion through this new port I have placed attention on the heart chakra where the line enters the body using both intention and attention to invoke "infusion" of much more than vitamin C. Once again I perceive this stage in my healing as a gift. Although I am still getting used to the catheter, checking it perhaps a little too frequently, and dealing with the body's stress reactions, I have this little theory that anything that causes me to remember God's grace (which this does time and again) has to be a good thing. So be it!

Catheter

Wow I laugh
As they nudge me
    out of anesthesia
I haven't been this fucking high
    since the 60s
That was 33 years ago
    I reflect
Surprised I can even subtract
Can I see it
I ask the surgeon
Sure
The nurse opens my gown
There it is
Not at all where
He said it would be
Not at all
Where I was expecting it
Under the right clavicle
Instead
It's smack-dab in the middle
    of my chest
Nestled between my breasts
There it is
Exiting through the center
    of my heart chakra
There it is
A delicate thin blue
Plastic tube
Coiling around the
    heart lotus
That grows up
    out of
The mud of unconsciousness
    and fear
Into the pool of Love
There it lays
Waiting for an infusion
    of Holy water

Healing waters
That will course through
    the veins
On their way to the front line
Reinforcements for weary troops
Warriors staring down cancer

Isn't God indeed
Curious and mysterious
For all practical purposes
This is a Groshong Catheter
    inserted into the chest
    due to poor venous access
    for the purpose of cancer treatment
For all impractical purposes
One might say
This is a reminder
That God will do
Whatever it takes
To infuse
The heart
With his boundless glory

Affirmations

By definition, affirmations are positive statements which succinctly language for us what we intend in our healing process. Quite simply put—they affirm. Affirmations replace old thought patterns with new. The discoveries being made in the mind/body connections in healing are indeed far reaching. Biofeedback, meditation, affirmations, visualizations are just a few of the mind/body techniques being investigated in cancer research as well as heart disease, arthritis and other chronic degenerative conditions. Though I tend to support the premise that cancer is a bit more complex than simply the result of negative thinking or repressed emotion, I do believe that a trustworthy shift from life-negative habits both (outer and inner) to life-positive habits is crucial to healing.

Typically affirmations are short, one sentence at best, with each word carefully chosen to enforce and reinforce the most positive possibility. They may be worded to target a particular mood, such as despair or fear. They may also be directed to a particular part of the body. They can *affirm* an attitude that is already present and strong in us, or serve as a positively stated response to some habitually negative thought pattern that we know is counterproductive to our healing. I use affirmations that fit each of these categories and some that fit them all.

A number of books offer listings of ready-made classic affirmations. Check your local library for more information. I must confess that the affirmations I have used have more or less chosen me. Some people might say they are a revelation of sorts. Call them what you will, the point is they are not positive statements that I thought up or read elsewhere. They belong to me. I hold them as sacred and very powerful.

I am very wary of some of the material I have seen on affirmations. It is my observation that affirmations filled with angels, rainbows and. "happy endings" are founded in illusion and often steer us away from the journey into real healing which is founded in "reality is reality"— nowness. Trust the wisdom of your own inner voice to direct you in your choice and use of affirmations.

Some people write their affirmations over and over in their attempt to reverse a negative habit. Again, trust yourself on this one. My personal experience is that trying to "drill it in" is counterproductive and tends to encourage poor self-image. It actually puts too much emphasis and focus on the negative image itself. Although I may not write my affirmations in repetitive practice I do often find myself internally repeating one numerous times in a day. (Of course this is contingent on the mood of the day and the condition of my mind at the time.) I do write my affirmations in my journal. Typically they are accompanied by insights that are imperative to record. They may pop up in my poetry as well.

You may find that writing your affirmations more than once at any given setting is helpful. You may go through a healing period, such as a chemotherapy cycle, where you find tremendous support in writing a particular affirmation each day before your treatment. I refer to the affirmations that have been crucial in my healing process again and again.

Remember, as with all aspects of *Writing Your Way Through Cancer*, simplicity, relaxation, authenticity and honesty should prevail. Please do not use affirmations to either escape or to complicate your own good sense of what is truly best for your healing journey.

Headwaters

I watched myself
Recklessly dive
Into headwaters of hope
Virgin springs bubbling
    with longevity
Tributaries leading to
Crystalline pools of promise

Young
    brilliant
Cancer doctor
Sitting at the source
Like Schweitzer
    at the mouth of the Nile

Bring your x-rays
    path' reports
        list of treatments
Pack in your IV equipment
We'll hook you up
Pump in some "C"
Take blood
Investigate
    analyze
        determine
We're high-tech here
State of the art
We cure cancer

I hung up the phone
Full immersion
At Lourdes

Belief
    faith
        trust
Are half the battle

Later
As I float downstream
Source at my back
I spy up ahead
Swirling waters
That precede
Cascading falls

From My Journal

June 1999

I awoke this morning to an affirmation: It's Just Cancer. I actually tried to think more about it, but the mind was literally locked onto the clarity of It's Just Cancer. There was nothing else to think, to analyze, to reflect upon.

Since that moment, when the tentacles of fear begin to creep in, I am able to take refuge in this realization of It's Just Cancer.

From My Journal

September 1999

The statement—"It's just . . . "—has been arising in different forms and circumstances for many months. Put into a larger perspective, it almost seems as though it is part of a momentum being built to give foundation to the truth of It's Just Cancer. For a while I've been responding to the attachment to movies as It's Just a Movie . . . or It's Just Chocolate, or even It's Just a CT Scan, It's Just . . . . Each time I have languaged this for myself or someone else I have felt the importance that we give to the material world disintegrate before me. Perhaps it's another aspect of confronting the reality of impermanence.

Things are just what they are. Some of the realizations that ride on the tails of the It's Just . . . understanding are:

> *It's no more than what It Is*
> *It is not separate from the whole*
> *It is not this or that*
> *It is not greater than or less than*
> *It is not right or wrong; good or bad*
> *There is nothing to conquer or defeat*
> *It (whatever it may be) is not a sign of anything*

As usual, these statements all seem to communicate the obvious. However, it's the light, the atmosphere they give rise to that defines these brief moments. The light is so sharp, so clear, so impeccable that I am able to return there and Remember.

Visualizations

Pac Man, Rambo, running water, golden light, piranha, laser beams, Darth Vader as well as Obi Won Kenobi are all visualizations I have used. In addition, I use all the elements: clouds, rain, sun, wind, even an occasional flood. Creative visualizations harness the healing potential of the mind. Through the process of bringing both our conscious awareness and inner attention to mental imagery we can actually use the power of the mind like medicine in our cancer healing. Scores of survival stories testify to the science of mind over matter. The fund of research substantiating the impact and effectiveness of visualizations in the field of cancer therapy has skyrocketed in the past few decades from the brilliant and seminal work of Carl O. and Stephanie Simonton to the more recent meditations of Jon Kabat-Zinn.

I don't think up visualizations. They seem to choose to "visualize me" much in the same way my affirmations arise. When a visualization presents itself I try to simply relax, then bring as much of my conscious attention to the image as I can. I try not to interfere too much with the natural flow, but rather use the power of the mind to compliment or co-pilot the organic movement. Of course, the challenge with visualizations is remaining focused long enough for it to do its work.

My own experience has been that some visualizations repeat themselves, allowing extensive use over time, while others are a one time thing. For example, when I was working with the Rambo image it was strong and pervasive for twenty-four to forty-eight hours...then *vamoose*—a bit like Rambo himself. Some people find it most effective to focus on one visualization and use it consistently for the same amount of time each day.

There are many healthgiving benefits to creative visualizations. They're free, have no negative side effects, can only do good. They can be used in conjunction with treatment. They enhance surgery and recovery. They strengthen remission. I believe that when needed they can even reprogram the cells.

I write my visualizations for reinforcement, I refer to them regularly, and I can literally feel the positive effects in my body. I have a tendency to either elaborate upon or dilute my experiences over time. Through writing my visualizations with as much clarity and simplicity as possible at the time they arise, I have an accurate description to refer to when re-engaging them. Writing them also strengthens their innate healing power.

From My Journal

April 1998

As I was drifting off to sleep a visualization arose that I have been using for the past week. I imagine a scintillating golden scarf. I wrap it around the tumor in a specific way so that the tumor is contained on all sides. I carefully lift it out of the body, gently place it on my altar, offer it up in prayer.

I visualize a beautiful golden light flowing like a river through my lymph system, my vascular system, the rest of my digestive tract; basically all through the body, brightening, cleansing, illuminating.

From My Journal

April 1998

The sky was robin's egg blue with a few clumps and wisps of clouds here and there. I began watching the clouds being blown around by this strong wind. I noticed a small cloud formation just overhead that was exactly the same shape as the tumor. I watched the wind blowing it, changing its shape second by second. It was like watching a slow motion film. I internalized the imagery allowing the wind and sun to slowly and gently break up the tumor's mass. Then, I began to feel that the disintegration was going too slowly. The cloud would change shape, but somehow regroup the next moment. Its outer edges would move all around to form new boundaries, but the core of the cloud seemed to become denser.

I wanted to stay focused on the image. I wanted to dissolve this moment of impatience, this desire to control my existence by even wishing to control the clouds. Of course, all this was a subtle internal process. I closed my eyes to this cloud formation for a moment, a brief moment, in order to simply bring my attention back to the breathe, to self-remember. Seconds later, I opened my eyes and the cloud had vanished. Totally. There was no trace of it or any part of it anywhere in the sky.

Of Cowboys and Cancer

Cowboys cut cattle
At sunrise
No quarter horses
No herd dogs
Just white hats in hands
They stand like bookends
Brothers
One waves his hat to keep
Confused cattle back
The other waves his hat
To
Keep
Excited cattle moving forward
They yell back
       and
           forth
In universal cowboy
Code
He-yah's   yip . . . yip
Git   they snap
Through kicked up dust
At dawn

The doctor said
See those cells with the
     bright green spots
They're lymphocytes
The green is a
Cancer Indicator
We watch
Eyes pressed to microscope
We estimate how many
I go home
Pray
Visualize them vanishing
Two months later
I watch
Healthy cells
Cut out

Green spots
Reject them
Send them back to the pen
Like cowboys
With white hats
At dawn

Telling The Story

At the risk of being ousted from the New-Age-Cancer-Support-Healing-Community I would like to suggest that telling "our story" over and over is not only unnecessary, it can also be potentially dangerous and counterproductive to our overall wellness and healing. I do think it is essential to tell our story, honestly and openly share our feelings, listen with vulnerability to our woundedness, forever reaching and relaxing into the possibility our story offers for transformation. Telling the story, your story with intention to release yourself from the past, to be vulnerable in your grief, to elicit compassion and understanding in relation to anger, jealousy, sorrow, despair, past resentments, and to reach out for nurturing in times of fear is purposeful. Telling the story to solicit sympathy, collude in feeling victimized, attract attention, or reinforce identification with cancer is unwise and indulgent.

It is very easy to get *stuck in the story*. Initially, it both feels supportive and is healing to tell our story, especially if we are lucky enough to share it with someone who really listens. It's crucial for cancer patients to be heard. However, the tendency, not only with cancer patients but with alcoholics, those with HIV, and a host of abuse victims is to become so identified with their "battle" that they wear their disease/recovery like a campaign button. Years ago I remarked to a friend with AIDS that when he introduced himself it sounded like this: "Hi. I'm Jack. I have AIDS." The truth was that he was also a best-selling author, a teacher and a student of numerous spiritual disciplines, among other things.

Writing Your Way Through Cancer is an opportunity to keep writing your *now.* Telling the story holds us to our definition of ourselves in the past, making a new definition for the present and future difficult to move into. Pay attention when writing to slipping into repetition of the story. Giving yourself ample time and opportunity to *really* tell your story in detail will help to reduce the inclination to repeat. Acknowledge your feelings both at the time of diagnosis as well as when writing about diagnosis. Apply this principle throughout your journey. There is no question that cancer is a very dramatic event. At times, you may feel like an entire Italian opera is being staged inside. At other times, a one-woman show. Whatever the case may be, write from your heart, your soul, taking risks, listening deeply to each and every voice that wants expression through your pen and paper.

Some events will automatically draw you back into the past. For example, at hearing the news of yet another death of someone who thought they had beaten cancer you may feel discouraged. This is a different exercise from telling the story. Another tip: pay attention to using the term *victim,* i.e., cancer victim. Assigning yourself the position of victim is not conducive to healing.

Most importantly, remember that cancer is only one part of who you are. Although it may often seem like a gigantic piece, it is really all in how you divide the pie. Write about your wholeness—your art, hobbies, children, grandchildren, the books you read, flowers you grow, lessons you learn, observations of yourself you like and those you hope to change. I am many things other than a cancer patient. I am a mother, friend, author, teacher, gardener, meditator, bike rider, reader, aspiring gourmet cook, poet, blues appreciator, and more. Writing about all of me helps to diminish the all-consuming nature of cancer, thus keeping things in perspective.

We don't need to identify our cancer when introducing ourselves anymore than someone needs to specify their race over the phone.

From My Journal

July 1999

With cancer you can't cover up your woundedness. You are suddenly exposed. Others may not be able to tell you have cancer by looking at you, however, you can tell by looking at yourself. This can be a beneficial thing. A great deal of energy can be expended in an effort to conceal woundedness. Many physical wounds heal much more quickly when they are left exposed to the air, the sun, the elements. This is true for emotional wounds as well. Exposure gives us a chance to see them for what they are.

Having the catheter tube exiting from my chest is a great example of this principle. It's visibility will not allow me to conceal my woundedness. Not really. Therefore, each time I access the port, I am able to come into relationship with that woundedness and make a gesture toward healing.

I think this inability for cancer patients to conceal their woundedness is one of the major reasons that cancer support groups have been so successful in aiding people in their journey to transformation. Once you confess your diagnosis to someone else with cancer there is an unspoken camaraderie that develops, almost instantaneously. There's a level of understanding and compassion that simply "IS." It may not be true relationship, or perhaps I should say lasting relationship, but there is an undeniable bond that is not mere sentimentality. It's more an awareness of the preciousness of time; the impact of the truth of our mortality; the intersection with the undeniable fact that there is a force in the universe that is greater than the individual will; the recognition that there is an organic desire or will to survive, and that physical pain is real.

Unfortunately, in telling the story we sometimes allow our common wound to encourage us to collude in feeling victimized, to mistake self-pity for self-nurturing, and to slip into identification with our disease.

These past months I've found value in exposing my woundedness to both myself and others. I have also found equal value in allowing those wounds to heal in the chamber of solitude.

Language

A well-meaning friend unconsciously said to me, when she heard of my diagnosis (which by the way was a year after my surgery), "far better you than me." She was attempting to compliment my courage, discipline and resilience. However, I was unwilling to have such a comment hanging out in the ethers. I responded to her statement in the moment with detachment and a matter-of-fact tone of voice, "No. It's not *far better* that I have cancer. And I know that's not what you meant." She wasn't offended and actually thanked me.

I have no qualms about correcting my doctors, nurses, surgeons, mother, child, neighbor or masseuse. The spoken word carries great weight. Of course, I don't censor nor make an issue of every negative, fatalistic remark I hear about cancer. If I did I would be miserable. I allow many unconscious words to float right by since I'm not willing to live in a state of paranoia. However, I am also my own greatest advocate. If I am to truly take and keep charge of my own healing, then I get to determine what gets said about it, at least when I'm around. Because I am sensitive to certain energies both positive and negative, it is crucial to me that the energy that surrounds my work with cancer be positive. It is more important to me to have a positively charged healing environment than it is to tip toe around the feelings of others (particularly health care professionals who are, for all practical purposes, strangers). Friends and loved ones wish to support me however they can, so ninety-nine percent of the time are grateful for my reminders. Given that healing is a system of reciprocity, my family reminds me when I slip into old patterns of negative speaking.

Writing Your Way Through Cancer can support us in how we language our journey. Once again, I am not speaking about making the hardships, grieving, pain, or shamanistic journey "nice-nice." I'm referring to choosing language that targets our feelings clearly, as opposed to labeling our worst fears. In the section on "Telling the Story" I reminded you to avoid referring to yourself as a cancer *victim*. Write about the implications of this example. Write about the distinction of referring to yourself as a cancer patient or cancer survivor. Another example might be to examine how you face and language the possibility of death. Feel the difference in "I'm probably gonna die," with "Death, which is part of life, may be the ultimate outcome of this encounter with cancer."

Consider what might be possible for many of us if we *never* heard the word terminal; if no one ever put a time limit on *our* lives; if we knew nothing of first stage, fourth stage and so forth. I'm simply inviting us all to consider the implications of self-fulfilling prophecies and the power we give language.

Write your way using intentionally chosen words that will impress your healing journey.

Scar

Two beautiful Spanish speaking
    black haired little girls
Point
    with wide-eyed wonder
At my scar
As I stand naked
With my little girl
    in the dressing room
        at the "Y"

Perhaps their 8-year-old minds
Are blank
Perhaps filled with images
    from horror movies

Not covering up
I mime
"It's where she came out"
This was true
I did not mention
That my uterus
Had been excavated
From that same
Cavern
Nor did I confess
That cancer had lived
Down in there
Beneath the zip line

It's been a year
Since the surgeon took his scalpel
To my lovely belly
And pulled out the tumor
That had been squatting
Uninvited
    in the warmth
      of my bowel
A swamp monster
Feeding off the refuse

The scar's still got
Numb places
Where there's no feeling
Whatsoever
Nerves severed
Central meridian
Still in shock

I love my scar
I wouldn't say
    I'm proud of it
But I do love it
For it reminds me
    that I am a
Survivor
That an angel was born
    of this body
As was a devil
Both
Bringing joy and grieving
In their placenta
Afterbirth
Filled with gratitude

This scar
Sings to me
Each morning
Sometimes a rich mellow gospel
Mahalia singing
"Sweet Jesus, I'm Alive
Praise the Lord, I'm Alive"
Other days
It's an angelic lullaby
Once I recall
Pavarotti passionately pleading
Something in Latin
    from *St. Matthew's Passion*
It speaks to me
Of the resilience
    of the human body
And the miracle of healing
The wonder of it all

My scar
Is sacred
    to me
A stigmata of sorts
A reminder
That out of suffering
Love is born
Ugliness can be transformed
Into Beauty
At any time
    in any moment

By the way
Those precious little girls'
Response was
"Cool"
Amidst giggles

After they walked away
My daughter
Lay her sweet fingers
Upon my scar
Beaming
"Mom" she said
"I like that
I came out of there"

Cultivating Silence

Writing Your Way Through Cancer is a fairly inexpensive ticket into the powerful healing chamber of silence. Since, on the most superficial level, most of us cannot write and talk at the same time, in order to accomplish our goals in our writing practice we need to observe a certain degree of silence. Our external surroundings may not always need to be silent, however. Some of my best writing over the years has been done in bars, cafés, train stations, playgrounds and even at Disneyland. Yet, as a general rule these days, I typically choose silence and solitude in which to write.

Many of us have grown up feeling uncomfortable with silence. As children we may have been accused of being rude, stuck-up, unsocial or anti-social, shy or a host of other shame-based characterizations simply because we understood, appreciated and treasured the innate gift of silence. Western society is practically founded on noise and distraction. Many homes have two or more TVs, a stereo for every family member, numerous computers—lap-tops and video game arrangements—cell phones, and fax machines, which all run simultaneously, making the enjoyment of silence virtually impossible. We seem to do most anything to avoid even a few moments of silence.

Silence is a crucible into which our deepest passions, prayers and sorrows can be poured. A crucible where, in turn, the alchemy of transformation can urge us to faster healing in many dimensions: physical, emotional and spiritual. Silence cultivates listening. One of ego's tendencies is to listen to someone with one ear while the other ear is listening to our own internal response, rebuttal, story. Silence teaches us to listen, *really listen* both to others and ourselves. A very astute healer I went to wisely professed that, "All healing is about simply following your heart." In order to follow our heart, we must first listen to it. This is a bit challenging if not completely daunting if the radio is blaring, the TV squawking, or we are always trying to get in the last word.

It is not uncommon for cancer patients to fear that they might drown in the well of silence. *Writing Your Way Through Cancer* is an invitation to drink from this well—crystal waters of clarity, healing waters of contemplation and to reflect on the purpose of our life—as it is—in the pool of this same silence.

Remember: Deep appreciation of the power inherent in silence can also encourage us to insist on a quiet, silent and reverent atmosphere in which to write. Self-respect and self-honoring actually encourages relationship and communion. Yelling at your children or shushing your mate to protect your silent "territory" is not conducive to healing, and more likely a reflection of isolation. On the other hand, if you are open you may discover, as I have, that friends and loved ones will be infected by your joy and relaxation in silence.

The Space Between

In the Hindu tradition the space between the in-breath and the out-breath is referred to as the Abode of God, the dwelling place of Being, non-action. This is the instant in which the needle on the scale arrives at balance. Harmony.

Living with cancer is often a roller coaster ride of extremes. Stretches of time when there is equanimity often seem short and infrequent. One of the most challenging "balances" to maintain is between minimizing the realness of our pain and struggling with exaggeration, complaint, self-absorption. We find ourselves caught in between the need to express our reality in coping with cancer itself—cancer treatment, fear of recurrence, adjustment to a host of losses from mastectomy or colostomy, to hair loss, weight loss and even job loss, to name a few—and the need to live all the rest of our lives: raise our children, have sex with our partner, continue our volunteer work, practice cello, play tennis, and perhaps put cancer on the back burner.

There's a fear that if we minimize the pain, rage and grief, our loved ones, co-workers and support team will never believe the insidious, often all-consuming, merciless nature of cancer. We are also afraid that if we tell the truth we will be accused of exaggerating, and consequently be disempowered. We also deeply fear feeding our illness with negativity while striving with angst to support our healing with positivity. We fear that if we share our pain others won't hear our gratitude and vice versa. In reality, validation for our experiences must arise from within.

Typically, cancer patients feel an array of polar opposites simultaneously: terror and trust, anger and joy, resentment and gratitude, pain and bliss. The space in-between these mirror images reflects our authentic self—the self that exists in and of itself, with or without cancer. "Regression," "recurrence," "early detection," "terminal," are all meaningless markers of time that are the function of *do-ing* as opposed to *be-ing*. *Writing Your Way Through Cancer* can be a doorway into this space between, the dwelling place of our deepest spiritual self, where it does not matter what anyone else's interpretation of our choices, coping mechanisms, pain threshold or perceived denial is about. Where there is no such thing as "terminal."

To be able to live in the space between we must release both ourselves and others from this desperate and impossible desire to believe us. Writing our experience with accuracy, absence of judgment, and focus will enable us to eventually rest in the space between, where validation is no longer an issue, either from outside or inside ourselves. Deep, lasting healing will carry us beyond validation into being with *what is*. Write your way there. Patience is key. Compassion begins with the self.

Life As Usual

Upon second diagnosis
The doctor asked
    Well, does this make you
        want to take a trip
           to the Greek Islands
    Kick up your heels
    Do something wild   ?

Not really
I responded

    It makes me
    Want to
    Live the life
        I have been given
    Consciously and fully
    In every moment   !

The doctor doesn't understand
You can't run away
From cancer

Celebration

One summer morning while visiting friends in France I was walking alone down their lovely wooded driveway; my daughter had just galloped off to play with her friends. A small white butterfly seemed determined to escort me down the lane. In short, the world worked. I remember having one of those moments of clarity whose message was "My life is perfect—just as it is." The mood was one of inner celebration. I walked on aware of how green the green was. Everything was bathed in the scintillating light of its own perfection.

Then my mind asked, "Gee, how can this be? You have this catheter hanging out of your chest, through which you will have to pump medicine later today because . . . " In that moment the mood of the celebration of life, my life, exactly as it was—cancer or no cancer— was so solid that it could not be affected by the mind.

Even in the worst scenario I have always found something to celebrate. Celebration is often a matter of viewing the world in all its perfection (and what we may wish to label imperfection) from the awesome perspective of the miraculous. In that moment in time on the lane, the mere fact that I was alive was indeed something to celebrate.

It's unfortunate that as a culture we have grown accustomed to celebrating mostly on predetermined dates that are often fueled by department store sales. There is an inner richness that is cultivated when we allow ourselves to spontaneously celebrate the simplest, most ordinary expressions of the wonder in our lives. Celebration is a mood. We may wish to celebrate the beauty of having lived another day by drinking a glass of carrot juice or green tea with greater intention for healing. We may throw a festive dinner party to celebrate a positive lab report.

Writing Your Way Through Cancer is a glorious tool for expressing celebration. Write about those ecstatic moments of joy, the small victories, even the rapture of really feeling your pain. Experiment with poetry, haiku or a dialogue with God.

Remember: Celebration does not negate the fact that some days just plain suck.

From My Journal
April 1998

Each morning upon waking, I turn to the absolute beauty of the ordinary. I witness the ordinariness of my life, which I have loved for so many years, literally glow with luminosity and become extraordinary. Even the most mundane task such as laundry has taken on this quality of extraordinary ordinariness. For example, the other day after speaking with the doctor, hearing a diagnosis of cancer, as I sorted the lights from the darks, checked my little girl's jean's pockets for forgotten treasures, spray-n-washed her undies, added the detergent, then straightened up the laundry room, each action was the expression of the ultimate beauty inherent in the simplest of tasks. In this moment of awareness, this ordinary task became a moment of prayer—a moment free from self-reference, free from cancer—free.

Haiku

Giant purple mums
   consume lungs
      leaving no room for cancer

Humor

One of the greatest adversaries for pain and suffering is humor. On the grossest level, a sense of humor can help us focus our attention on something else, carry us out of self-reference and into a broader perspective. On a deeper level, I believe that laughter and a sense of humor can literally mend damaged tissue and repair broken hearts.

By humor I don't mean cynicism. I'm referring to humor that enables us to see the paradoxes that exist all around us. Humor that brings tears of laughter. Humor that encourages us to feel. When I awoke from anesthesia after my fourth surgery, I literally burst out laughing. The loss of time I experienced while unconscious was positively hysterical to me—a paradoxical moment in which I was clearly aware of our (human beings') bizarre relationship to *time.* My next proclamation, exclaimed through guffaws, was, "Shit, this hurts!" On the way home from the hospital I rented a stack of comedy videos, which I watched over the next few days. Though I was in so much physical pain I had to sleep sitting up for days, I never took a pain pill (which I do use when I need to without a trace of guilt). This genuine mood of humor escorted me graciously through my pain for quite some time.

Writing Your Way Through Cancer can be an inroad into cultivating a friendship with humor. Norman Cousins literally made a science of laughter as a means of dealing with pain and disease. Cultivating a sense of humor or strengthening an already strong sense of humor is crucial to our healing. Try writing a Dave Barry-like piece about some aspect of your treatment. Or, keep a list of jokes, or simply put on the attitude of finding humor in the most distressing situation and writing about what you see.

Cancer is a *serious* matter but we don't always have to take it so *seriously.*

No Ice Cream   or   Ode to Carrot Juice

Drink it until your skin
Turns orange
The more orange
The better
I drink
    I drink
        I drink
I look at the palms of my hands
I'm sure I see a yellow tint

Just say no to
ice cream cakes brownies
chocolate chip cookies dates raisins
jam honey apple juice hamburgers
hot dogs chicken sausage
    and
        and
           and
Eat your broccoli sprouts
They're great
Anti-cancer food
And make sure you get in
chard argula beet greens
pumpkin and deep yellow and
green leafy vegetables

And didn't you read that
Fresh
    (organic of course)
Raspberries
Reduce tumors in rats
And brown rice and millet
And seaweed dulse kelp and
    arame and kombu and nori
        and
           and
              and
Green tea

Why can't cancer cells
And ice cream get along

Stage 3. Transforming
Through Cancer

From My Journal

June 1998

Several days ago I was rubbing some ointment into my incision scar. I paused to look at myself in the mirror. Whew whee! That's some scar! For an instant I felt mutilated. Not so much from the standpoint of vanity, but invaded, vivisected, opened up, cut. I stood there naked, transfixed by the scar, until I felt the atmosphere around me begin to shift. Then I began to experience the scar, the wound, as something much much more symbolic and useful. I know little about the Jungian archetypes, or even about mythology. But somehow in that moment, I felt I was receiving what I might loosely define as "transmission." Now, I cannot even begin to language this transmission, because I do not know the words to give it. What I do know is that there was a new found feeling of the possibility that lies in the scar, in the wound, in the very act of having been cut open, in having organs taken out. Something like a sacred rite, the path of the wounded healer. Something about the shamanistic journey; something about the scar being a very ancient scar, a universal scar; being cut open down the front meridian, something about being cut open through a major chakra. Something about the immense possibility within such a profound reminding factor.

I could probably research all this, but I almost don't want to intellectualize the potency of the transformational possibility in such a wound—a necessary wound.

Dignity

Following my cancer surgery I was placed in a semi-private room. I had thirty-two staples in my belly. I had just received the news that the tumor had penetrated the colon wall. A pathology report would be forthcoming. I was very raw, emotionally, and still dopey from the anesthesia and pain medication.

A curtain divided the room. A friend sat with me reading as I drifted in and out of sleep. On the other side of the curtain the TV blared, while what sounded like a dozen people seemed to shout at the tops of their voices. After a while the cacophony died down and then the only sound I could hear was what I gathered to be an elderly woman lying in a clinitron bed which is used to prevent bed sores. It made a mesmerizing, rhythmic hum.

A nurse brought in dinner for the woman and helped her move to a chair, which happened to be within arm's reach of my head. There she sat, quietly eating her dinner. There I lay silently praying, only a sheer curtain between us. The noisy relatives had all gone, and the sound of this faceless old woman simply chewing her food was so comforting to me. For, in the midst of this frightening turn in the labyrinth of my life, her chewing reminded me of the beauty possible in ordinariness. This ordinariness soothed me.

Then, Boom! The loud family returned, blasting into the room, harshly interrupting my reverie. They began to nag the old woman about finishing her food, treating her like a child, commanding her to finish her pears—arguing with her when she said she didn't like them. "Yes you do mom-mom. You love pears." And so forth. This harassment seemed eternal. My tears began to flow. These people were robbing this wise elder—who had unknowingly soothed my wounds with her organic simplicity—of her dignity. Ultimately, this all too common situation served me by opening a floodgate of emotion regarding my own situation. It christened my journey into the realm of cancer with a tacit realization that it is my human right to be treated with dignity regardless of the level of dependency or need I might be in along the way. This intention colored my entire hospital stay, and how I related to nurses, lab technicians, high-powered surgeons and the house-cleaning staff—and them to me.

Dignity may be a challenge to feel when we are bald from chemo, integrating a prosthesis after mastectomy, learning how to live with colostomy, sporting a Groshong Catheter™ for IV treatment, or hooked up to morphine due to unbearable pain. Society at large has an extremely narrow definition of dignity which influences our acceptance of ourselves and our condition at a deep level. There is also a quite Victorian attitude that at once and completely confuses dignity with "acting dignified."

Out of necessity most of us have had to reach beyond our limited view of ourselves to ask for support in our healing process. Having cancer forces a level of vulnerability that many of us have guarded all our lives. To suddenly find yourself on your hands and knees vomiting after a round of chemotherapy creates a vulnerability that is hard to match. Feeling your own sense of dignity in the face of others' responses, no matter how well intended, is an awesome task. Being condescended to, pitied or doted on does not contribute a lot to healing, though it may serve vicariously, as it did me, to boost us into warriorship—to perhaps stand face-to-face with healthy indignation.

Being treated with dignity begins with self-respect, self-honoring and acceptance. *Writing Your Way Through Cancer* automatically enhances our sense of dignity. It encourages a healthy sense of pride. Writing can help us stay in touch with situations or relationships which threaten our sense of dignity—situations in which we feel treated like children who need decisions made for them; children who haven't the vision to know what is best in their own healing. Quite often we aren't aware of those improprieties until we view them in retrospect. Writing encourages self-reflection. It gives us a chance to say, "Hey, wait a minute. That's not what *I* want. It's what *they* want." Healthy indignation supports us in reclaiming our own truth. Regardless of the circumstances, every human being on this earth has a right to be treated with dignity.

Try writing an essay on dignity in the face of cancer.

White Geese in Northern Germany

One thousand geese doing
Salutations to the sun
One thousand geese
    with beaks pointed south
Eyes sharp with fear and longing
One thousand geese
With their wings cut
Aching to take

f   h t
  l   g
    i

To fall into formation

They try to fly
Instinct tears through their
Wing stubs
Clouds and blue skys
Pierce their hearts
Gentle wind beckons
    "Rise up
        Soar"
"Come" she teases
"Spread your wings
    and glide upon my tresses"

Instead
They skim across the dirt
Stumble in the mud
Nestle into the rain-pocked earth
Waiting
For salvation

Their destiny is plain
The farmer arrives
In stove-pipe rubber boots
And an army-green slicker
Rifle to his eye
It's Christmas
One thousand humans

Need their Christmas goose
  POW

It's so simple
For the farmer
To take a life Y
   A_W A

From a dirty white goose
Whose dignity has been stolen

It's so simple
For a microscopic cell
To grow out of control
To reproduce
Like imprisoned geese

Waiting

Life as we know it begins with waiting. We wait in the deliciousness of the womb to be born. As newborns we learn very quickly that there are times when our needs are gratified immediately, and other times in which we must wait. We have to wait until we are *old enough* for what seems an eternity. Great literature is filled with metaphors for waiting. Many of us feel we ultimately wait for death and the promise of renewal.

I have come to define waiting as an art. This definition was born out of necessity, for my life has been colored by hating to wait. Typically I would change lines at the grocery, change lanes in traffic, sigh and grumble at the dentist, threaten to leave at the doctor's, fidget, bite my nails, beg someone to let me go ahead, stomp off. When I allow myself to enter into the quiet, still place inside, waiting transforms from sheer aggravation to something holy. The waiting itself allows space for reflection, deepening preparation. When I am plagued by impatience, nervous anticipation or tension, the possibility inherent in waiting is lost and the activity is relegated to a stress-filled waste of time.

Cancer offers us endless opportunities in which to practice the art of waiting. On the simplest level we wait at the doctor's office, wait for a nurse to return a phone call, wait for an insurance authorization, wait for a surgery date. On a deeper level we wait for a pathology report, CT scan result or a pain reliever to take effect. Anxious waiting at the doctor's office is most likely quickly overcome the moment our name is called. In contrast, waiting for the results of a CT scan can catapult us into a veritable hell realm of anxiety, dread, ill temper and strained relationships. We feel we are waiting for the answer to our destiny.

The art of waiting in the deepest sense is a spiritual journey. In the Hebrew tradition at Passover, the Feast of Seder is observed. A chair is left empty in hopes that Elijah, the Awaited, will appear. The waiting is celebrated. Intention is foremost. Preparation is sacred. We wait for the answers to prayers. We wait for miracles. We wait for visions. We wait for union. Eventually we wait for death. We can wait anxiously, unconsciously. Or we can practice the Art of Waiting.

Writing is a priceless canvas in the gallery of the Art of Waiting. Lessons, understandings, revelations wait to be discovered. Writing gives these gifts a wall to be hung upon for viewing. Writing is also an opportunity to practice waiting. I wait for inspiration, the right word to come, and completion. When I wait I try to remember to let my breath guide me. The breath is quite seasoned in the art of waiting.

To learn this art, try bringing your journal or note pad to the doctor's office. (One of my latest little missions is to inspire physicians to install a writing table in their waiting rooms.) Write about how you're feeling, especially if you are kept *waiting*. The next time you catch yourself pacing in anticipation of that phone call—write. Sit down and write. Keep some scrap paper by the phone so you can write while the insurance company has you on hold. Write while waiting for the plane, dessert, IV to finish, your son or daughter's Aikido lesson to be over. So often, while waiting for a blood draw, x-ray or some other invasive procedure to be "over with," I have written my way through anxiety, impatience, discouragement, into clarity, tolerance, relaxation, joy.

Loneliness, Aloneness, Solitude

I watched a movie about Mother Teresa many years ago in which she spoke about her work, saying that it wasn't the lepers in India nor the homeless in New York City whom she found to be the most challenging to serve, but rather the lonely. Loneliness is a state of existence in which we choose not to feel our organic and sacred connection to the whole of the manifest world. Loneliness is an attitude which can be equated with separation, isolation, and self-absorption. Loneliness is a type of dis-ease, an illness. For the one who is plagued with loneliness is indeed not well, not feeling whole, but rather empty. I have read numerous accounts of cancer patients who describe or label their situation as one of loneliness. My hunch is they were lonely long before a diagnosis of cancer.

Aloneness is an entirely different situation. I believe that each of us has a specific work to do during our lifetime. This "work" is unique to us, cannot necessarily be done by anyone else, and requires that ultimately we must go there alone. This aloneness does not isolate us. In fact, if I accept the truth that I am the only one who can inhabit this physical body, pursue its/my unique path, die my own death—not lonely mind you, but indeed alone—then universes of relationship, communion, connectedness and community become available. When I am in denial of this truth I repeatedly find myself desperately trying to enlist my loved ones into doing my work for me. Comfort, compassion, listening from the heart, wisdom, all respect the path of the lone warrior. In turn the lone warrior understands the principles of bondedness, reciprocity and a code of honor.

Aloneness can be a tremendous refuge. When I take refuge in my aloneness I create a space for solitude. Out of the mood of solitude beauty and mystery are illuminated. When I rest in solitude my loved ones feel included, even invited into the stillness. It is attractive, invocational. Sometimes the atmosphere is rarefied, but more commonly it is simply rich in ordinariness. In this sacred space there is no room for loneliness, self-pity or isolation. Prayer abounds; poetry is unencumbered; listening is implicit.

Writing Your Way Through Cancer is an invitation to inquire into the parts of you that use the excuse of loneliness to escape the grit of relationship. Check out if you run from the truth of aloneness because you fear death. Do you avoid solitude because it may be a catalyst for real feeling? It is possible to write your way out of loneliness into the sanctity of solitude. I know because I have done it. Remember, we must write our way through many of these situations over and over. Growth is ongoing. Change is constant. The next time you feel lonely—pick up your pen.

From My Journal

June 1999

Loneliness arose as a teenager. Loneliness, I knew, had been there since the womb. Loneliness was a result of lack of bonding, the incubator, not being breast-fed. Loneliness went underground after birth and infancy; then gurgled up like a hot spring during adolescence, with acne, gawkiness and poor self-regard.

Coincidentally or not, the first poem I ever wrote, as a teenager, was about this subject.

> *Solitude*
> *Coupled by a fear of the unknown*
> *Colored by shades of the past*
> *Illusions of what the present*
> *Seems*
> *I wished so for the rain*
> *   and darkness*
> *And when it came*
> *It comforted me*
> *And so I sat and watched the rain*

This mood of loneliness seemed to evaporate with high school graduation. College brought with it a new world of friends, an insatiable hunger for learning, the awakening of self-discovery. For the next twenty-five years I virtually forgot about loneliness until cancer began to unearth "It" all . . . Until a recommendation came from one of my healers to "make some distinctions between loneliness and aloneness."

Deeper investigation revealed both a genuine love, if not passion, for solitude coupled with some unresolved issues with loneliness. Through being willing to face the truth of the loneliness, I was able to see the truth of the search for solitude and the love of solitude growing in the same garden as the loneliness. I was also allowed the sweet opportunity to feel some compassion and forgiveness as opposed to pity for this lonely wounded teenager who was also being gifted through that wound. The garden is a beautiful garden. A garden of Gethsemani; a sanctuary for prayer, communion and true worship.

Through becoming friends with the loneliness (trite but true), I can fall into even deeper intimacy with solitude. I can enter the silence without fear, walking into even deeper recesses within the cathedral of the Divine. Sometimes I wonder if I would have eventually wound my way into this chamber in the catacombs of the Spirit without cancer.

Prayer

Prayer is a tricky subject. My personal experience of prayer is that the healing process is greatly enhanced by the power of prayer. In some instances I believe it is the cure. I put great stock in the domain of mystery and miracle. I am not referring to the domain of "hocus pocus"; rather the domain in which the non-linear, unexplainable healing (which perhaps is all healing) takes place.

Prayer has gained a lot of credibility in the past decade, particularly in the field of cancer treatment. Oncologists, surgeons and pediatricians specializing in cancer are engaging in an array of clinical trials using prayer as the experimental control. Terminal cancer patients who have ceased all other treatment to await death have suddenly experienced spontaneous remission they would or could not attribute to anything except prayer. In some instances, this prayer was not even done by them, but rather by the church congregation, the members of their synagogue, or friends and relatives. In some cases, the patients had no knowledge of these prayers even being offered.

Writing my way through cancer has been a form of prayer—an appeal to God as well as a vehicle through which to give thanks; a chance to walk with God through the greatest challenge I have faced.

Prayer is a spiritual expression which enables me to keep perspective; to remember that this occurrence has more to do with spiritual healing than "strengthening my immune system." Prayer is crucial in the effort to create an environment in which spiritual transformation is possible. And spiritual transformation is surely a result of grace, not will, although it requires us to be accessible, vulnerable, and willing. Prayer can help us move out of the position of aloneness into the crucible of solitude.

You may wonder where *Writing Your Way Through Cancer* and prayer intersect. For some, this intersection is a meeting of affirmation and inquiry. Initial questions such as *Why me? What am I living for? What is death? What is the soul? How can this feel like a blessing?* can and often do lead to answers that can only be revealed through prayer, faith and trust in a higher purpose. Such questions cannot be fully answered with the mind, but rather catapult us into the realm of the miraculous, the un-understandable, the mystery.

These internal investigations are the true heart of the process revealed in *Writing Your Way Through Cancer.* The answers found here are the substance of the path of transformation and healing. If you find spontaneous prayers arising you may wish to write them down. Remember, the writing itself can ultimately lead you into the heart of prayer, as well as become the prayer itself.

Of Blackberries and Nettles

Symbiosis
Exists
In nature
For a reason

In order to pluck
    a succulent blackberry
From the forest in Northern Germany
You must reach
Through the nettles

You must either
    avoid   or
    reel   in
The rapture of its sting

It's the same with
    cancer
        and
    gratitude

From My Journal

May 1999

A scrumptious dessert was served tonight—all my most favorite ingredients: fine bittersweet chocolate, marscapone, whipped cream. Heavenly. Of course I didn't have a bite. They say, "Cancer thrives on sugar." There is no disagreement about this fact. I am blessed with discipline, so I won't eat the sugar, but tonight it was hard. I made mint tea instead. I let myself cry a little. Funny, it was so very little—one tear rolling down my cheek in slow motion.

At first it was a tear of self-pity. At first, just about all I could think was how my life is different now. Vows such as "no sugar" are serious. "No sugar" could give me a few more months of life. Oh it's certainly not the only factor I must look at here, but they all come together to make a complete picture. It's gesture, discipline, Intention. So as this tiny tear of self-pity moved farther along, it moved into the dimension of transformation.

What started out as self-reference, self-pity, sorrow and even anger evolved within the space between in-breath and out-breath. "No sugar" became a gesture of sacrifice to the Divine: a very small sacrifice actually, in light of the immensity of blessing and grace and gift that is perpetually showered upon me. And, suddenly, my heart was filled to overflowing with the sweetest nectar one could imagine—so much sweeter than any dessert could ever be.

Service

Time and again I have been literally lifted out of the rising well of despair and discouragement through service—simple acts or gestures which draw me out of my "small" self into my "big" self by allowing me to put others' needs first. Service is a system of reciprocity. When we serve from the heart we often feel fed, energized, complete. Serving others can touch us deeply because it often opens up the channels to compassion, empathy and gratitude. When I give, I always get more in return. Even when what I receive sometimes invites me into feeling my pain, this too I consider a gift.

Being a parent carries with it a built-in invitation to service. One might compare it to being like an all-night supermarket—open every day including weekends and all holidays, where the customer is always right, and all returns, refunds and exchanges are honored. Attempting to serve our families while in the throes of treatment can be excruciating at times. It can also be the only life raft in sight. Inviting my daughter to lie next to me so I could read to her while I did an IV at home gave me an opportunity to serve her while struggling. It simultaneously softened some of the "scary stuff" for her, even if on a subconscious level. On low energy days, I found such healing joy in cutting a mango just the way she liked it, as opposed to dwelling on the dinner I was too exhausted to prepare. Serving our families is one obvious arena for service. There are countless others.

Service is different from martyrdom! True service arises out of wholeness, being both a contribution to our healing and a result of our healing. If you feel drained, resentful or apologetic after "serving," then you most likely have been rescuing or "martyring."

In *Writing Your Way Through Cancer* you can remind yourself of the authentic gift of service. Try writing about the ways you have been touched both by serving and being served. You may wish to serve your loved ones by sharing some of your poetry or reading aloud a particularly poignant piece of journaling. *Writing Your Way Through Cancer* is an act of service to your own healing as well as that of others.

A small reminder: Allow yourself to *be* served regardless of the stage of your illness or the degree of need. Service can be welcoming those who love you to share in your process.

From My Journal

June 1999

On the international flight I look into the eyes of the woman on our aisle. She's from Albania, a country torn by war, ravaged by ethnic pogroms. In her eyes I see the suffering of all of humanity. Yet she smiles each time I glance her way. Her smile is rich and deep with no trace of self-pity, nor any trace of blame, hatred or victimization. She asks us to help her figure out the headphones . . . the disembarkment card. Each time we help she smiles sincere gratitude and warmth. I feel dwarfed by such sweet dignity in the face of immense cultural suffering.

Rebirth

Many cancer stories tell the story of birth or rebirth that arose out of a gestation period of suffering and pain, grief and loss, despair and discouragement. A realized life is a life of dimension. There are many shades of suffering—from the Holocaust and the Oklahoma City tragedy, to the grief inherent in miscarriage or a diagnosis of cancer.

Living with cancer, regardless of the ultimate outcome, seems to have the innate possibility of redemption and rebirth. Cancer patients share stories of pain and isolation being transformed into gratitude and renewed communion with family and loved ones. Lives previously characterized by selfishness dissolve into the beauty of service and self-lessness. After diagnosis, greed, ambition and competitiveness may fall away as contentment, philanthropy and a relaxation into the marvel of simplicity gather momentum. Most cancer patients who share these experiences wholeheartedly confess that given their previous track record and the direction their lives were taking prior to diagnosis these transformational changes would most likely never have occurred without cancer.

It is not always easy to be graceful, grateful, and hospitable to pain and suffering. Even if we know intellectually that redemption may await us on the other side, relaxing or letting go into that very suffer-ing is not always an easeful process. After all, society is obsessed with pain relief—from ibuprofen to morphine, from movies to the Internet. Our culture is not encouraged to "be with our pain" or "feel into our suffering." *Writing Your Way Through Cancer* has the potential to either gracefully ease us down into our heartbreak or jar us into observing our desires to escape at all costs.

When my father was in the hospital dying of cancer he continued to smoke cigarettes. After all, he knew his illness was irreversible, so why bother to work on breaking a lifelong smoking habit at this point? Wasn't he entitled to some small comfort considering the level of his suffering? Considering the fact that he was going to die? He was already in so much pain; why add yet another aggravant?

It's not my intention here to judge my father's choices. My father smoked to distract himself from pain, the fear of death, the loss of a longer life (he was fifty-eight), the confrontation with any regrets he might have had, and the abuse that showed up in his behavior during the last years of his life, and so on. Apparently, he saw no other options.

My father and I had few conversations during his last months, so I am sad to say I really know nothing about his transformative experi-ences approaching death. What I do know is that I experienced a mood of softness I had not felt in him since I was a child. After my father's death my brother came across a small stack of poetry my dad had written as a young man. Apparently he was quite prolific at one point. I wonder what might have been possible for him in his healing and final moments of life had he chosen to check out of the hospital, go home and take up his poet's pen.

Rebirth in the context of healing is not necessarily about gaining more time in the literal sense. However, it is about gaining time in the deepest, most profound, spiritual sense. Transformation is never a waste. If truly feeling our pain and suffering allows us to go deeper into the breakdown of our attachment to the material plane, i.e., the very playing field of this suffering, then the potential breakthrough or rebirth that awaits us on the other side, even if in the eleventh hour, is actually a small price to pay. It is also a testimony to the possibility of *bending time* in the truest sense.

Perhaps before his death my father quietly, invisibly returned to the deep spirituality revealed in his poem *To Dusk*, which he had written as a young Navy man in 1945. My writing it certainly makes it a more real possibility for me as I heal something for us both.

To Dusk

Oh Dusk Thou'rt Queen—the night and day to rule,
With Crown so filled with early diamond Stars;
What Peace be found upon Thy flowing Breast,
What rich Devotion o'er the angry years.

Oh Dusk, oh Dusk, when Day hath had her fun,
And every face toward hearth of Home hath turned,
Thy quiet and pleasant smile of strength doth run
To soothe each heart, each soul, which Day hath burned.

Oh Dusk upon Thy face can e'er be seen
The Light of Nature's passionate embrace,
The Wind Thy brush, the Rain to wash Thee clean,
Thy garment clouds each in its given place.

And quick Thou'rt gone to end another page
Within Life's Book; but once again I've trod
The Heights of Grace, and did all Truth engage;
I saw Thy Face—and saw the Face of God.

—Otis Knox Martin, Sr.

From My Journal

May 1998

I've been thinking about how we go through cycles of spiritual births and deaths. I have gone through numerous gestation periods, feeling pregnant, aware that some gift of God was coming my way. In these circumstances I was usually unsure of just what would be born. Impregnation by the Divine is not a predictable thing. One can't simply arrange an ultrasound to determine the gender of the "being" about to emerge. At other times I haven't even really been aware I was pregnant, about to give birth, until I was in labor. Sometimes these spiritual pregnancies are incredibly easeful with a miraculously short labor. Sometimes, it seems, the due date will never come, and once in labor it's painful, frightening and I want to run away.

A few days ago I had an ironic thought that this recent "pregnancy" issued forth as a whopping baseball-size malignant tumor. One never really knows what the Divine may bring for one's work, or why, for that matter. And one certainly cannot decide within the first few days, weeks or even months how the "child" will develop, what lessons will be revealed.

Forgiveness

For most of my adult years I *struggled* to find forgiveness. I knew that the roots of present physical as well as emotional dis-ease were entangled in old tap roots of blame and resentment. I was sure forgiveness could untie these knots and heal some wounds, but no matter how hard I "tried," forgiveness evaded me. A wise friend suggested I relax, stop trying so hard. Astute advice. Relaxation revealed knots of anger and sorrow embedded in the earth of unhealthy shame over my "failure" to forgive.

Following my cancer diagnosis it became obvious to me that the person I needed most to forgive was me. It was also clear that forgiveness is not a function of effort, but rather an unfolding. Forgiveness is also an act of grace. In order for forgiveness to find its way into healing, there needs to be some "letting go."

Writing Your Way Through Cancer is a process whose very foundation is one of letting go and accepting. Once we begin to really accept the truth that our life has actually been perfect, and that no one is to blame for the hardships, crises, losses and even the tragedy, the road to forgiveness and the possibility it offers stretches out before us. Growth can take place.

Internal courage and personal integrity is required on the journey into acceptance. Writing is a direct route into this awesome and sometimes frightening domain.

There is no "how to" with forgiveness. Even so, its very nature is transformational. If we relax and accept, it will unfold in its own time.

Forgiveness

I fell into a stream of
Forgiveness
Waters of compassion
Gently carrying away
Debris
Scars
Being rubbed smooth
By the steady flow
 of tears
That tasted
Like mountain dew
Cold
From lifetimes of
Melting snows

No thing
 can cling
For ever
In rushing waters
Sooner or later
Even the steadfast
 boulders of blame
Must break free
To tumble
Over the crystal falls of change
To rest
In pools of
New beginnings

Death Is Not A Failure

I think about death and the mystery of what awaits after death. Sometimes my thoughts are informed by fear; at other times by excitement. Sometimes all I can see is the face of my ten-year-old daughter and I am at once overwhelmed with an indescribable blend of emotions—from ecstatic love and trust in God's Divine Plan for both of us, to a grieving so deep there seems no bottom to this well of heartbreak. In most circumstances I prefer to use the term "transition" when referring to death of the physical body. Transition implies continued growth, evolution—change. Death implies an end.

Cancer is not a punishment, but rather an opportunity. Death is not the booby prize—though it can certainly feel that way, especially to those of us who planned to live a bit longer. Some of us will live with cancer for many years; some of us will be cured; some of us will die soon after diagnosis. All of us will be touched in some way as a result of being challenged by cancer. Each of us will eventually die to what we call *life*. Some of us will suffer miserably, others will simply slip away. For the most part, when facing these issues I have come to the conclusion that death is the least of it. It seems that it's really what we do while *alive* that makes the difference in how we die.

One of the most difficult and insidious aspects of healing is the belief that we all should be able to cure our cancer; that if we just wanted to bad enough, prayed hard enough, visualized enough, we could beat it and be one of those victorious survivors rather than one who just didn't have the right intention.

Death is not a failure, however. As far as I'm concerned, the "failure" is the belief that we have done something wrong to create our cancer, and the belief that we have failed by not curing it. We cannot possibly live life to the fullest if we are plagued with such guilt.

Write about death and transition. Write letters of gratitude (whether you send them or not is up to you) to your loved ones, or to someone who touched your life whom you never thanked. Explore your fears. Encourage your wonder. Make a list of your attachments that it would be helpful to let go of. Write a dialogue with God. Try some poetry that expresses grieving. Allow *Writing Your Way Through Cancer* to help you relax into *what is.*

Food for Worms

    Get into the coffin
      says the Zen master

What does it mean
                  to become
Food for worms
Pondering impermanence
I ask
What is left   of this body
After the worms
Have their fill
Where is the soul
What is emptiness
How will I pray
    with no flesh
          no heart

Cease your questions
    I shout
Get into the coffin
    I sing
Greet death
With hands folded in salutation
Willingly lay yourself
Upon the banquet table
Invite the worms, the maggots
To celebrate
Your transition
Insist
They lick your bones
Clean
Then
Be off with you
Skip into your new life
    with bells on your toes
Prayer on your lips
And gratitude in your heart

Stage 4. The Unknown

From My Journal

The issue of giving up control also seems ludicrous, for indeed there are ways in which I never feel a sense of control at all.

There is, no doubt, a striking contrast between the times of immense acceptance that opens into rivers of gratitude for the ongoing opportunity to challenge each and every stagnant attitude, belief system, as well as fear, and the unavoidable plunges into the desire to totally escape reality—a reality laced with pain.

Lately I am able to observe, while drowning, that I am drowning. This act doesn't always increase my aptitude for treading water; however, it does radically decrease the panic, thus making it possible for me to see the lifesaver when it is thrown out to me. I am in water much too deep for me to be able to swim in (literally and symbolically), but it is the depth God has placed me in. And so far, bit by bit, He keeps me afloat.

The Mystery

A close friend shared the story of her grandmother's breast cancer. Diagnosed at the age of sixty-two, the woman politely thanked the doctor, marched home and resumed her already comfortable life without making a single change. "I'm an old woman," she said. "The good Lord will take me when He's ready." She never bothered to have another x-ray, buy an antioxidant or stop eating junk food. She lived with a huge tumor growing on her breast and died at ninety-seven from a stroke. At a recent visit with my surgeon he said, "When cancer patients ask me how much time they have I answer 'That's up to God.' "

I have read accounts of cancer patients who attribute survival solely to the power of prayer. Some claim chemo saved their lives. Others swear by shark cartilage and carrot juice. Some of the most heartwarming, inspiring tributes have been written by spouses who escorted their loved ones through every possible treatment, life style change and path of courage they could manage. Many of these cancer patients died in spite of their efforts.

Through writing my own healing journey I have come to realize that whether we have cancer or not there are no guarantees. There are vast elements of my personal life as well as all of creation which must remain a mystery.

The human ego wants to be in control. In order to maintain control one must have the answers. Having all the answers essentially negates the mystery—the place in which there are no predetermined answers. The place from which anything can happen.

Giving up control, trusting, surrendering, letting go, can all be frightening at times. It's also been my experience that beneath the fear lies a mood of relief and gratitude. If and when I can release my grip on the vision I have of my future, then I am able to rest in the present. The future simply unfolds with unpredictability and awe. When this mood occurs I am also able to see that everything I have encountered thus far in my life—all of it, including loss, abuse, misfortune, illness—has been placed in my path to teach me a lesson. This realization exonerates blame and resentment as well.

Sometimes I sense the irony in spending tremendous amounts of time, money and energy to heal, while at the same time attempting to relax, release, trust—that is, to surrender to "what is" without giving up, to trust in a higher purpose without falling prey to complacency, to remain passionate, positive and responsible while remaining vulnerable and open. Cancer is a worthy opponent, as Castaneda's don Juan Matus would say. It forces us to confront the mysterious.

Writing is a doorway into realms of mystery, irony, pathos, contradiction. Let your pen guide you there.

From My Journal

May 1998

During the surgery the doctor removed the tumor, re-sectioned the bowel, removed the gall bladder, removed the appendix, removed a cyst on the ovary, and removed twenty lymph nodes that looked suspicious. All of this had to go to pathology to be biopsied. It would take three to four days to get the results. The results came in yesterday: six of the twenty lymph nodes were positive. The tumor had penetrated through the wall of the bowel.

According to the experts I still have cancer. I cannot be considered cancer-free because the cancer could have metastasized to other locations. It's an interesting place to be left in—with questions left unanswered; not knowing for sure if there is cancer in the body or not. The doctor says, "Whether there's cancer left in the body or not, we don't know. Given the percentages . . . most likely yes. And, it is purely possible that we got it all. The fact is, there's no way of knowing at this point."

Years ago a wise teacher said to me, "You have to learn to live without resolve." At the time he was referring to having disagreements with my friends and loved ones. However, today that advice comforts me. For in order to be what nothing can take root in, to draw no conclusions, I must be able to live without resolve. Resolve is not necessarily a bad thing. It's just that the need to feel resolve about everything interferes with Trust.

From My Journal

May 1998

It was such a blessing to be lying here with tubes and needles in every conceivable opening; nurses poking and tugging; thermometers, blood pressure cuffs, and have the mind and heart repeating:

Beloved Father
Surrender me to Your Will

From My Journal

October 1998

Since the cancer I have traveled through many a dark night over this issue of who's in charge. It's so easy to slip into the new-age trap of believing we can change our own destiny, we can "heal/cure" ourselves of any and everything that befalls us. We really want to believe at all costs that we are in charge, that ego will survive, that we are ultimately immortal.

We do all we can do. The rest is up to God. Sooner or later we must give it all up, let go of it all, and put it in God's hands.

Without the Great Trust, the small trusts are shallow, and often weak. The Great Trust subsumes habitual doubts and fears. The Great Trust is a state of Being, and the small trusts are usually a result of effort and will. I have experienced, time and again, that I cannot will myself into a real place of resting in Trust. It is Gift. In fact, it almost feels like It is "Trusting" me—not Trusting In me—but Trusting the me that is the expression of It. So the Trusting in this small self or cell becomes part of the matrix of the greater Trusting, which is the Divine itself.

Ravishment

My father's body was ravished by cancer. He was almost unrecognizable by the time he died. The disease of cancer has a distinct personality, you might say. One quite different from heart disease or Alzheimer's. Some cancer patients do not encounter extreme ravishment, however many do. A state of being raped of energy, appetite stolen, the sacred house of the body and soul being broken into and plundered.

Ravishment is a difficult state in which to find joy and gratitude. However, ravishment is the very foundation for spiritual longing. Ravishment may indeed strip the body of its flesh. It can also take with it greed, competitiveness, jealousy, avarice, selfishness and pride, in turn leaving us raw, open, vulnerable to energies and dimensions that we are typically either guarded against or too busy to be bothered with. When our defenses are gone and we haven't the strength to keep our psychological rackets intact, the light of the Divine can pierce us as well as envelope us.

Although I have not experienced the physical ravishment that may appear in the last months of life, I have felt an aura of ravishment that has left me hungry for this piercing light of longing and vulnerability.

Writing can help ease us into the arms of ravishment and lay us gently into the lap of the Divine.

OTHER TITLES BY CHIA MARTIN

WE LIKE TO NURSE
by Chia Martin   Illustrations by Shukyo Lin Rainey

Research has documented that the advantages of breastfeeding far out-
weigh the disadvantages in the overall health of the child. This unique
children's picture book supports that practice, as it honors the mother-
child relationship, reminding young children and mothers alike of their
deep feelings for the bond created by nursing. Captivating and colorful
illustrations present mother animals nursing their young. The text is simple
and warmly encouraging.

*"A delightful way to remind the very young of our species' natural heritage as
well as our deep kinship with other mammals."* —Jean Liedloff, author
Continuum Concept

Paper, 36 pages, 16 full-color illustrations, $9.95 ISBN: 0-934252-45-9

• • •

ROSIE, THE SHOPPING-CART LADY
by Chia Martin   Illustrations by Jewel Hernandez

This book tells what happens when a sensitive little boy confronts the hard
reality of a dishevelled old woman who wanders the city streets collecting
trash or treasures in her shopping cart. It addresses neither the global
questions of injustice nor a specific solution to the massive problem of
homelessness in the U.S. today. Rather, easy-rhyming text and colorful
illustrations highlight a story designed to inspire questions and conversation about this important subject.

*"This heartwarming story is a reminder of the need for each of us to become
involved in our communities. It is never too early to learn the message contained in* Rosie.*"* — Elaine L. Chao, President and CEO, United Way of
America

Hardcover, 32 pages;   ISBN: 0-934252-52-2
16 full-color illustrations, $15.95

**TO ORDER PLEASE SEE ACCOMPANYING ORDER FORM
OR CALL 1-800-381-2700 TO PLACE YOUR ORDER NOW.**

OTHER TITLES BY CHIA MARTIN

THE ART OF TOUCH: A Massage Manual For Young People
by Chia Martin
Photographs by Sheila Mitchell

Provides young people (ages 9 and up) with a simple, step-by-step method for learning massage techniques to use on themselves and others for relaxation, pain relief and increased self-esteem.

    Encourages a young person to respect his/her own body and the bodies of others, and: * Assists them in finding "center"—a place of inner harmony and inner balance.* Introduces the mind-body connection which lies at the root of an holistic approach to health. * Invites young people to view touch as a gift as well as a form of healing.

"Chia Martin's book views children as capable, interested and effective in the healing 'arts.'" —Ashisha, Managing Editor, *Mothering Magazine.*

Paper, 60 pages, 92 photographs, $16.95   ISBN: 0-934252-57-2

TO ORDER PLEASE SEE ACCOMPANYING ORDER FORM OR CALL 1-800-381-2700 TO PLACE YOUR ORDER NOW.

ADDITIONAL TITLES OF INTEREST FROM HOHM PRESS

AFTER SURGERY, ILLNESS, OR TRAUMA
10 Practical Steps to Renewed Energy and Health
By Regina Sara Ryan,
Foreword by John W. Travis, M.D.

This book fills the important need of helping us survive and even thrive through our necessary "down-time" in recuperating from surgery, trauma, or illness. Whether you are recovering at home or in the hospital for a few days, weeks, or even months, this book will be your guide to a more balanced and even productive recovery. It follows a wellness-approach that addresses: managing and reducing pain; coping with fear, anger, frustration and other unexpected emotions; inspiration for renewed life; becoming an active participant in your own healing; dealing with well-meaning visitors and caregivers...and more.

Paper, 285 pages, $14.95   ISBN: 0-934252-95-5

• • •

THE WOMAN AWAKE:
Feminine Wisdom for Spiritual Life
By Regina Sara Ryan

Through the stories and insights of great women whom the author has met or been guided by in her own journey, this book highlights many faces of the Divine Feminine: the silence, the solitude, the service, the power, the compassion, the art, the darkness, the sexuality. Read about: the Sufi poetess Rabia (8th century) and contemporary Sufi master Irina Tweedie; Hildegard of Bingen, author Kathryn Hulme (*The Nun's Story);* German healer and mystic Dina Rees, and others. Includes personal interviews with contemplative Christian monk Mother Tessa Bielecki; artist Meinrad Craighead and Zen teacher and anthropologist Joan Halifax.

Paper, 20+ photos, 518 pages, $19.95   ISBN: 0-934252-79-3

TO ORDER PLEASE SEE ACCOMPANYING ORDER FORM OR CALL 1-800-381-2700 TO PLACE YOUR ORDER NOW.

ADDITIONAL TITLES OF INTEREST FROM HOHM PRESS

10 ESSENTIAL HERBS, REVISED EDITION
by Lalitha Thomas

Peppermint. . .Garlic. . .Ginger. . .Cayenne. . .Clove. . . and 5 other everyday herbs win the author's vote as the "Top 10" most versatile and effective herbal applications for hundreds of health and beauty needs. *Ten Essential Herbs* offers fascinating stories and easy, step-by-step direction for both beginners and seasoned herbalists. Learn how to use cayenne for headaches, how to make a facial scrub with ginger, how to calm motion sickness and other stomach distress with peppermint. Special sections in each chapter explain the application of these herbs with children and pets too.

Paper, 395 pages, $16.95   ISBN: 0-934252-48-3

• • •

10 ESSENTIAL FOODS
by Lalitha Thomas

Carrots, broccoli, almonds, grapefruit and six other miracle foods will enhance your health when used regularly and wisely. Lalitha gives in-depth nutritional information plus flamboyant and good-humored stories about these foods, based on her years of health and nutrition counseling. Each chapter contains easy and delicious recipes, tips for feeding kids and helpful hints for managing your food dollar. A bonus section supports the use of 10 Essential Snacks.

Paper, 300 pages, $16.95   ISBN: 0-934252-74-2

• • •

TAO TE CHING FOR THE WEST
by Richard Degen

A new rendition of the revered classic, *Tao Te Ching*, this sensitive version offers a contemporary application of Eastern wisdom to the problems created by modern Western living. This highly-readable collection presents a way of life characterized by harmony and integrity; a way that bypasses the happiness-depleting traps that people of all ages have set for themselves and others.

Paper, 120 pages, $9.95   ISBN: 0-934252-92-0

TO ORDER PLEASE SEE ACCOMPANYING ORDER FORM OR CALL 1-800-381-2700 TO PLACE YOUR ORDER NOW.

ADDITIONAL TITLES OF INTEREST
FROM HOHM PRESS

MANAGING AND PREVENTING PROSTATE DISORDERS
The Natural Alternatives
by George L. Redmon, N.D., Ph.D.

Well-established and current research indicates that prostate disorders are largely preventable, and for those already afflicted its symptoms are manageable by a wide variety of natural means. This book about prostate health contains lifesaving information that every man, and his family, should know about
- Who is at risk?
- Prevention options
- Safe, natural treatments for prostate disorders, including, * nutrition and dietary recommendations * enzyme therapies * energy medicine * highly effective herbs and supplements *detoxification programs and more.

Contains a complete Resource and Referral Guide

Paper, 220 pages, $12.95   ISBN: 0-934252-97-1

• • •

THE JUMP INTO LIFE: *Moving Beyond Fear*
by Arnaud Desjardins
Foreword by Richard Moss, M.D.

"Say Yes to life," the author continually invites in this welcome guidebook to the spiritual path. For anyone who has ever felt oppressed by the life-negative seriousness of religion, this book is a timely antidote. In language that translates the complex to the obvious, Desjardins applies his simple teaching of happiness and gratitude to a broad range of weighty topics, including sexuality and intimate relationships, structuring an inner life, the relief of suffering, and overcoming fear.

Paper, 216 pages, $12.95   ISBN: 0-934252-42-4

TO ORDER PLEASE SEE ACCOMPANYING ORDER FORM
OR CALL 1-800-381-2700 TO PLACE YOUR ORDER NOW.

ADDITIONAL TITLES OF INTEREST
FROM HOHM PRESS

UNTOUCHED
The Need for Genuine Affection in an Impersonal World
by Mariana Caplan   Foreword by Ashley Montagu

The vastly impersonal nature of contemporary culture, supported by massive child abuse and neglect, and reinforced by growing techno-fascination are robbing us of our humanity. The author takes issue with the trends of the day that are mostly overlooked as being "progressive" or harmless, showing how these trends are actually undermining genuine affection and love. This uncompromising and inspiring work offers positive solutions for countering the effects of the growing depersonalization of our times.

"To all of us with bodies, in an increasingly disembodied world, this book comes as a passionate reminder that: Touch is essential to health and happiness."—Joanna Macy, author of *World as Lover, World as Self*

Paper, 384 pages, $19.95   ISBN: 0-934252-80-7

• • •

SIT: *Zen Teachings of Master Taisen Deshimaru*
edited by Philippe Coupey

"To understand oneself is to understand the universe." – Master Taisen Deshimaru

Like spending a month in retreat with a great Zen master, SIT addresses the practice of meditation for both beginners and long-time students of Zen. Deshimaru's powerful and insightful approach is particularly suited to those who desire an experience of the rigorous Soto tradition in a form that is accessible to Westerners.

Paper, 375 pages, $19.95   ISBN: 0-934252-61-0

TO ORDER PLEASE SEE ACCOMPANYING ORDER FORM OR CALL 1-800-381-2700 TO PLACE YOUR ORDER NOW.

ADDITIONAL TITLES OF INTEREST
FROM HOHM PRESS

THE WAY OF POWER
by Red Hawk

Red Hawk's poetry cuts close to the bone whether he is telling humorous tales or indicting the status-quo throughout the culture. Touching upon themes of life and death, power, devotion and adoration, these eighty new poems reveal the poet's deep concern for all of life, and particularly for the needs of women, children and the earth

"This is such a strong book. Red Hawk is like Whitman: he says what he sees..."
William Packard, editor, *New York Quarterly.*

Paper, 96 pages, $10.00   ISBN: 0-934252-64-5

• • •

MARROW OF FLAME: *Poems of the Spiritual Journey*
by Dorothy Walters
Foreword by Andrew Harvey

This compilation of 105 new poems documents and celebrates the author's interior journey of *kundalini* awakening. Her poems cut through the boundaries of religious provincialism to the essence of longing, love and union that supports every authentic spiritual tradition, as she writes of the Mother Goddess, as well as of Krishna, Rumi, Bodhidharma, Hildegard of Bingen, and many others.Best-selling spiritual author and poet Andrew Harvey has written the book's Introduction. His commentary illuminates aspects of Dorothy's spiritual life and highlights the "unfailing craft" of her poems.

"Dorothy Walters writes poetry that speaks to us from the heart to the heart, gently touching our deepest spiritual stirrings."—Riane Eisler, author, *The Chalice and the Blade.*

Paper, 144 pages, $12.00   ISBN: 0-934252-96-3

**TO ORDER PLEASE SEE ACCOMPANYING ORDER FORM
OR CALL 1-800-381-2700 TO PLACE YOUR ORDER NOW.**

RETAIL ORDER FORM FOR HOHM PRESS BOOKS

Name _____ Phone (____) _____

Street Address or P.O. Box _____

City _____ State _____ Zip Code _____

	QTY	TITLE	ITEM PRICE	TOTAL PRICE
	1	10 ESSENTIAL FOODS	$16.95	
	2	10 ESSENTIAL HERBS	$16.95	
	3	AFTER SURGERY, ILLNESS AND TRAUMA	$14.95	
	4	THE ART OF TOUCH	$16.95	
	5	THE JUMP INTO LIFE	$12.95	
	6	MANAGING & PREVENTING PROSTATE DISORDERS	$12.95	
	7	MARROW OF FLAME	$12.95	
	8	ROSIE, THE SHOPPING-CART LADY	$15.95	
	9	SIT	$19.95	
	10	TAO TE CHING FOR THE WEST	$9.95	
	11	UNTOUCHED	$19.95	
	12	THE WAY OF POWER	$10.00	
	13	THE WOMAN AWAKE	$19.95	
	14	WE LIKE TO NURSE	$9.95	
		SUBTOTAL:		
		SHIPPING: (see below)		
		TOTAL:		

SURFACE SHIPPING CHARGES

1st book $4.00

Each additional item $1.00

SHIP MY ORDER

☐ Surface U.S. Mail—Priority   ☐ UPS (Mail + $2.00)

☐ 2nd-Day Air (Mail + $5.00)   ☐ Next-Day Air (Mail + $15.00)

METHOD OF PAYMENT:

☐ Check or M.O. Payable to Hohm Press, P.O. Box 2501, Prescott, AZ 86302

☐ Call 1-800-381-2700 to place your credit card order

☐ Or call 1-520-717-1779 to fax your credit card order

☐ Information for Visa/MasterCard order only:

Card #_____–_____–_____–_____ Expiration Date _____

Visit our Website to view our complete catalog: www.hohmpress.com

ORDER NOW! Call 1-800-381-2700 or fax your order to 1-520-717-1779.

(Remember to include your credit card information.)